SHELLEY

SHELLEY

or

The Idealist

by

ANN JELLICOE

FABER AND FABER
24 Russell Square
London

First published in mcmlxvi
by Faber and Faber Limited
24 Russell Square London WC1
Printed in Great Britain by
Latimer Trend & Co Ltd Plymouth

PR
6060
. E5 S5
c.3

TO ROGER

'I still inhabit this divine bay, reading Spanish dramas & sailing & listening to the most enchanting music. . . .'

FIRST PERFORMANCE

Shelley was first produced at the Royal Court Theatre on 18th October 1965 with the following cast:

Lead	RONALD PICKUP
2nd Lead	JOHN CASTLE
Older man	SEBASTIAN SHAW
Heavy	IAIN CUTHBERTSON
Walking Gentleman	TIMOTHY CARLTON
1st General Utility	BERNARD GALLAGHER
2nd General Utility	WILLIAM STEWART
Leading Lady	FRANCES CUKA
Juvenile Lead	KIKA MARKHAM
2nd Leading Lady	AVRIL ELGAR
Juvenile Character	LUCY FLEMING
Walking Lady	NERYS HUGHES

Directed by Ann Jellicoe
Designed by John Gunter

CAST

This play was written for a company of actors. The parts should be distributed as follows:

MEN

The Lead:	*Shelley*
2nd Lead:	*Hogg, Trelawny*
Older Man:	*Coplestone, Godwin, Lord Eldon*
Heavy:	*Walker, Westbrook*
Walking Gentleman:	*Master, Bailiff, Edward Williams*
1st General Utility:	*College servant, Westbrook servant 1, Moneylender 1, Eldon's clerk 1*
2nd General Utility:	*Beggar, Westbrook servant 2, Godwin's servant, Porter, Moneylender 2, Eldon's Clerk 2*

The two last change settings

WOMEN

Leading Lady:	*Mary Godwin, Miss Ferney*
Juvenile Lead:	*Harriet Westbrook*
2nd Leading Lady:	*Miss Pybus, Eliza Westbrook*
Juvenile Character:	*Hellen Shelley, Mrs Godwin*
Walking Lady:	*Miss Meeks, Jane Williams, Clare Claremont*

PREFACE

In my first play *The Sport of My Mad Mother* character and motive were shown in action not described in words; to give a simple example instead of a man saying 'I'm angry', he was angry. This seems more obvious now than it did ten years ago when theatre was still much influenced by Shaw and T. S. Eliot, both extremely literary dramatists. *The Sport of My Mad Mother* began with a fragment I wrote in which youngsters cavorted around a college-bred American teasing, tormenting, losing control and finally, as their ecstasy rose to a climax, passing out with hysteria: the words they used were meaningless sounds to release emotion. I looked at the fragment and asked: 'What sort of people would behave like this?' and so began to build character and then: 'What would such people do?' And began to build situation. I was interested in piling up patterns of sound and releasing them, and this taste dictated the play: it was about people who behaved like that because that was the way I wanted to write.

The Sport of My Mad Mother was a critical failure sharing the same fate as other plays of the time such as *The Birthday Party* and *Live Like Pigs*. But almost inadvertently I had found that I could write comedy (I'm thinking of the scene where Cone tries to persuade Fak to betray Greta). My training and background had always made me suspect, even be a little fearful of comedy: it was inferior to tragedy, and involved a mysterious and inexplicable skill which I didn't understand and couldn't share. Now after twenty years in the theatre a door opened, I was delighted. I wrote *The Knack* partly for the same reason as Shaw wrote *You Never Can Tell* and Ibsen *Love's Comedy*: to make sure of getting a play produced after an early one had failed. So *The Knack* is a comedy with four characters and one set, but I wrote it mainly because I wanted to explore comedy, to write a play that should be full of joy, innocence and zest.

The Knack, like my first play, was written from the inside, character determining situation, situation defining character. The

13

principle that action is not narrated was developed further. In *The Sport of My Mad Mother* the characters were incapable of understanding their own motives; in *The Knack* Tom sees clearly what motivates him and the others. Colin needs help but Tom sees danger in giving him ready-made answers; instead he tries to put Colin into situations where Colin will be able to recognize the nature of his problems and perhaps find his own answers; this is in contrast to Tolen who is always giving Colin good advice which weakens Colin and makes Tolen feel powerful. The man who understands seldom makes a direct statement, the others reveal themselves through what they say and do. The play is about how you should treat other people, and its form reinforces what it has to say. Speech rhythms are more subtly used than in *The Sport of My Mad Mother*; but there are interlocking rhythms which, with the youth of the characters and their zest, give the play its bounce. I was, however, beginning to be bored with verbal rhythms used in an obvious, musical way as they were in the first play, and to feel they were a mannerism.

Watching *The Knack* in performance I made what was for me a new observation on the way imagination works in the theatre. The play went on tour before it came to London. In Cambridge with an undergraduate audience, the play looked hilarious; in Bath, where *The Knack* was coldly received by small, elderly audiences, I was worried because the play appeared obscene; in London watching with a sophisticated audience, including a number of film people, the play was innocent. It was brought home to me that even I, the author, could not see the play in isolation. It is not simply that one's reaction is *coloured* by a particular audience, it is that—according to the nature of the audience—one sees a totally different play. The more self aware among us know that we often try and rationalize subjective judgments. We may say: 'That's a bad/dull play' when what we may really mean is: 'That play challenges certain ideas of mine either about art or morals that it would disturb me to have to change; so rather than admit that the play may be right, which would mean I'd have to re-examine my ideas, I will rob the play of its power by dismissing it as a bad play.' We know, too, that if we have to work hard at this suppression, we generate a kind of heat—anger against the play possibly disguised as virtuous indignation. But how many of us realize that without there necessarily being any change in the text or the acting, a play that was bad when we saw it in Bath last Wednesday may be quite splendid when we see it in London next Monday?

There are objective standards in the theatre—a play may be truthful, forceful, original and well-constructed—but in performance these standards are blurred and confused by the subjective influences at work among the audience. If an audience enjoys a play that doesn't mean it is automatically a good play, but it does mean that while a novel say, may be judged by an individual, there's no such thing as an individual reaction in the theatre. This seems to me to have some significance, for instance in relation to the 'objective, individual judgments' of newspaper critics. It gives new depth to the word 'entertainment' which is derived from Old French *entre* + *tenir* meaning literally 'to hold between'.

Soon after the production of *The Knack* I saw the Royal Court Theatre Studio working with tragic masks. If the story captures your imagination so that you begin to identify with the masked character, you would swear that the expression on the mask changes. In a given situation the mask begins to smile—a mask cannot smile and yet it smiles. The only explanation must be that one projects one's imagination on the mask to a degree one would never have suspected and would not have thought possible. The mask smiles because the audience imagines it smiling. If imagination can make a rigid piece of papier mâché smile, what can it not do? What is the limit to the power of imagination in the theatre? Another, related, observation: watching *Philoctetes* at the National Theatre I was struck by my reaction to Hercules' bow, at one moment it was merely as a well-made stage property, the next, my imagination having been caught, it became a magical object to be handled with care and reverence. Here one comes back to more familiar ground: the dichotomy that is the essential theatrical experience. You identify with the actors and yet you remain yourself: 'I am the Prince of Denmark yet I am also *me* sitting here in my seat.'

'Theatrical' began to have a further meaning for me. It used to mean tinsel, glitter, artificiality; it had come to mean in my first two plays the tension that arises from the conflict between what people say and what they do; but now 'theatrical' began to mean,

15

purely and simply, the actors catching the audience's imagination and the effects that follow. Everything seemed superfluous beyond the fact that once an audience begins to identify they will clothe the play with their imagination; anything that goes beyond catching the audience's imagination by the simplest means is unnecessary and vulgar; the audience is there with its unique theatrical function, beside this salient fact everything else seems mere frenzy. All I wanted now was to capture the audience's imagination and then take it somewhere.

My dislike of surface decoration grows. Everywhere, on television, on the radio, in magazines, the cinema and the theatre, there is a rococo concern with triviality, a taste for highlighting the odd, off-beat moment so that it appears significant; this is intriguing at first but it soon becomes tiresome, a refusal to face the real significance of life. All the popular mass media of communication are concerned to discover or create and capitalize the newest image, the newest person, the newest fad. This is having its effect on art, we are becoming too concerned with form for form's sake, we are being pushed into a kind of desperate smartness. We, the new writers, are being constantly compared with each other to see who is best, who is ahead, like horses in a steeplechase. This may be fine for the *Daily Express* and the Sunday supplements but it's bad for art and artists.

The success of *The Knack* in New York and as a film has freed me to follow what path I choose, at least for the time being. But I begin to feel alienated (temporarily I hope) from a society which has adopted *The Knack* and, it seems to me, subtly degraded it: a New York reviewer was able to write of the film that it was all the better for the elimination of the moral values in the play. *The Knack* is about the people who seemed to me most fresh and interesting at the time I wrote it. Society is always more or less on the boil, and every so often it throws up an image with which a particular group of people can identify and which they will use to shape themselves. James Dean and Jimmy Porter were examples of such images. At the pace we're going there seems to be an important new image every four years or so; the chief one at the moment is probably that of the model girl/fashion photographer/Ad Lib crowd. These people seem to me less kind, less warm-hearted, more concerned with money than were those earlier groups I wrote about in my first plays. I don't feel attracted to them and I don't want to write about them; after all it means months, as it were, in their company. There are other groups in our society, less immediately smart but also less ephemeral, in whom I am more interested. Has there ever been a time when more people were questioning the whole basis of morality, not merely trying to be moral but asking what morality is?

It was becoming clear that I wanted to write a play that would have a strong narrative. I wanted to do without vocal rhythms. Although in my earlier plays vocal rhythms were an organic part of character and situation, they seemed now to betray an anxiety to hold the audience's attention, and I wanted to see if I could hold it without them. Instead of a spinning web of shifting relationships, I wanted to build a story which would proceed step by step, each action drawing upon itself inevitable social consequences which would dictate the next action. Thus the characters in the play would be led to the point where they would have to make a choice. It frequently happens in the theatre that a play is built towards a choice and in the event the choice is evaded or cheated either because the dramatist doesn't know what he's doing or because he's afraid that the consequences of choice might be too uncomfortable, might disturb the audience. I wanted a remorseless progression towards a choice, the choice to be made, its consequences to be explored. Finally I wanted a given narrative which would provide me with a story that I should have to re-tell; instead of building a story from the inside, moulding it to the demands of my style, I wanted to mould my style to the demands of the narrative.

A combination of circumstances led me to read a biography of Shelley. I found that his life illustrates certain problems which fascinate me; particularly the problems of goodness which are so much more interesting than those of evil. Evil tends to run in grooves, evil men more or less conform in their evil; but goodness can be very subtle once you concede that goodness doesn't begin with a set of rules but with the search to define its own nature. Shelley's life involves, too, the problems of the creative artist rejected by his time, of the position of women, of the teacher who projects his own standards on his pupils and is disturbed when they don't live up to his image. Finally, while I agree with almost every word that Shelley says, I often find him engagingly comical because he was inexperienced, enthusiastic and intense.

He was young and I'm always attracted by youth: the pattern of life is not yet laid down and yet what we do in youth tends to decide the whole course of our lives. A fearless, joyful, serious man, his life touchingly illustrates how pathetic are our efforts to confront life, for the stones on which we fall and bleed are our own flaws projected forth. Life is impossible; but we have to struggle: for our own self respect, to keep back the tide of evil, to vindicate mankind. Shelley is a tragic hero insofar as he was a great man destroyed by his own tragic flaw: his blindness to the frailty of human nature. And he fulfils another definition of tragedy: he outraged the moral law of his time (and possibly of our time) and so, for our security, he had to be punished. Shelley worked out his own definition of goodness, his own ideals, but they were based upon abstract logic and reason and came increasingly into conflict with the realities of human nature, until the point was reached when those involved were liable to be deeply hurt. To save them pain, should he compromise?

The search into his life was delightful; at first through biographies but soon entirely from original sources. I now well understand the charm of writing biography: the pleasures of imaginative detection; the ease with which one moves, as it were, unseen amongst the great figures of the past in a way impossible with one's contemporaries not merely because one might not know them with that intimacy but because one cannot see the pattern of the time, its relationships as a whole. There was, too, a real delight in finding how English was this man who battled against what he disliked in England; and so a rediscovery of one's own Englishness. Selecting the episodes of his life and arranging them dramatically implies stress and bias and so it should; this is a play not a work of scholarship. But I tried to extract the truth of his life while stressing the points I wanted to make; events are sometimes telescoped but they are true to their inner nature (for example the events that led up to his first marriage). Where I have been most free, because the facts are not known, is in his final relationship with Mary. It is known that there was trouble. Trelawny's evidence that Mary only really appreciated Shelley when she had lost him, Shelley's own veiled

18

remarks, and Leigh Hunt, a kind and tolerant man, refusing to give up Shelley's heart to Mary after the burning, all show that in the eyes of their most intimate friends Mary had behaved badly. Shelley's poems, his nature, and Jane's claims in later life are evidence that the situation shown in Act Three Scene 1 is not without foundation. The great attraction of the theatre, and its difficulty for a writer, is that things happen moment by moment and the playwright must show them happening. He can't just indicate that they happened, as in a book, by saying, 'It was Mary who first declared her affection to Shelley'; the playwright has to show this happening or else put it into the mouth of another character reporting the event, in which case it's still action although in terms of another character and another situation. My desire for an extremely simple style imposed on me the need to present these events directly.

The form of the play continues to intrigue me. In an earlier draft the Older Man (played at the Royal Court by Sebastian Shaw with immense distinction) was called the Villain. He was seen in direct and scarcely-veiled conflict with Shelley; possibly Shelley's age or a little older, dark, irresponsible, free-ranging, evil. As well as the Older Man's parts he would also have played Miss Pybus and, as an irresponsible act, simply to rile Shelley, Eliza in Act Two Scene 1. This would have been in pantomime dame style and would, of course, have shifted the whole nature of the production. (It would also have called upon another aspect of theatricality: the challenge to the imagination, the joy of connivance. An audience that accepts an actor as Prince of Denmark gets a peculiar joyful release from accepting two men in a cloth skin as a pantomime horse.) I altered the Villain to the Older Man because, as I said at the time: If I dare I want the whole play to be utterly simple. But I would like to see this tried sometime. I would also be interested to see the play performed in modern dress.

My ideas continued to change and develop—not, one hopes, for the sake of change, but because it's rather boring to know what one will do next. The purpose of this essay was to trace the line of development from *The Sport of My Mad Mother* to *Shelley*, and I think it's fairly direct not only theatrically but in content; there is a link between Dean and Tom (or Tolen) and Shelley. It seemed necessary to do this because some critics have asked why I wrote *Shelley*. I write slowly and my plays appear at fairly widely-spaced intervals; I tend to cover a lot of ground in my theatrical thinking between plays and I suppose it must be disconcerting to find that I don't pick up where the last play left off but a bit further on.

I expect I shall go on exercising my freedom to write serious plays or frivolous plays, to develop or consolidate. I write for four reasons: for the pleasure of creating something, for the exhilaration of defining and trying to answer certain problems, because writing is a process of self-discovery and self-enrichment, for the joy of communication. This last is a continuing satisfaction: at this moment while I write there is a matinée of *Shelley* at the Royal Court Theatre; it's half past four, they will have reached Godwin's big speech in Act Two Scene 4. In the same way I sometimes wake early in the morning and think: 'It's nine o'clock in New York, they will have started the second act of *The Knack*.' It's the pleasure of communication, and each time it's a different communication because it's a different audience.

ANN JELLICOE

Richmond
November 1965

ACT ONE/SCENE ONE

BEGGAR.

Enter SHELLEY, 18 *years old, tall, fair-haired,*
gangling; reading as he walks and at the same time
eating cherries out of his hat. He drops a coin in the
Beggar's tin and walks on. Returns, gives the beggar
a handful of cherries, walks on.
Enter HOGG.

HOGG Shelley! Shelley!

SHELLEY Oh—Hogg!

HOGG There you are. I've been looking for you all over
Oxford.

SHELLEY What?

HOGG We arranged to meet in your rooms.

SHELLEY We arranged——?

HOGG Yes.

SHELLEY How extraordinary. Listen! I've been writing.
Listen!
'Yet, human Spirit, bravely hold thy course.'

HOGG Human Spirit hold thy course.

SHELLEY 'Let virtue teach thee firmly to pursue
The gradual paths of an aspiring change.'

HOGG Aspire to change.

SHELLEY 'For birth and life and death, and that strange state
Before the naked soul has found its home,
All tend to perfect happiness.'

HOGG For birth and life and death
All tend to happiness?

SHELLEY 'O happy Earth! Reality of Heaven!'

SHELLEY } 'O happy Earth! Reality of Heaven!
AND HOGG } Thou consummation of all mortal hope!

SHELLEY Of purest spirits thou pure dwelling-place!'

HOGG Earth. Earth. Earth. Earth.

SHELLEY 'Where care and sorrow, impotence and crime.'

HOGG Earth. Earth. Earth. Earth.

SHELLEY 'Langour, disease, and ignorance dare not come.'

HOGG Earth. Earth. Earth. Earth.

SHELLEY
AND HOGG } 'O happy Earth, reality of Heaven!'

(*An explosion. The stage fills with light.* BEGGAR *exits hurriedly*)

HOGG What was that?

SHELLEY An experiment, one of my experiments!

HOGG In the open street?

SHELLEY It wasn't meant to go off until I got back to my rooms. I'm afraid I got a bit excited and it ignited.

HOGG Let's go and have some tea.

SHELLEY You don't want tea.

HOGG I do.

SHELLEY Have a cherry.

HOGG No, thanks, tea.

SHELLEY Oh very well—oh.

(*They feel drops of rain*)

HOGG D'you think it's going to last? It's getting heavier.

SHELLEY Shall we make a dash for it?

HOGG Let's shelter under that tree.

(*They retire to one side and eat cherries*)

SHELLEY Fruit and rain! It's enough to make you believe in the divinity. You know when I argue with my father about the existence of God, he says I must believe because he, my father, says I should. He says if I believe in God I'll go to heaven, if I don't I'll go to hell. The Bishop used the same sparkling logic in a sermon last week; the carrot and the stick. How dare they so insult the divinity of man?

HOGG You really believe that men are divine?

SHELLEY The man who acts, not because he's been told such action is right, but because he knows it is good— that man is true to his divine nature. What's the matter?

HOGG Can I have another cherry?

SHELLEY Just let me make my point. Reason. Men must

22

reason! Governed by reason, governing themselves by reason! Sublime and inexorable! Cast off our slough of misery. Great, good, joyful, beautiful and free! Gods!

HOGG You're getting wet. If we were to import free food to feed the starving poor, do you think that the farmers would listen to reason?

SHELLEY Not yet, because the farmers do not know how to reason. They cannot see beyond their own narrow interests. But reason would tell them that the good of all is the good of each: teach them to reason and they will be reasonable. Free food, that's an interesting idea. . . . Hogg! What is it that makes food *food*? And some land fertile, some barren. Suppose we could find a chemical substance which would change the nature of barren soil. . . .

HOGG I don't agree with you about the farmers.

SHELLEY But you must agree that if you teach men to reason they will behave reasonably—you must educate people to see the truth. Look at those clouds! Racing! Flying! Balloons! The dirigible! What potential. I tell you, Hogg: the shadow of the first balloon that crosses Africa will emancipate every slave and annihilate slavery for ever!

HOGG Maybe.

SHELLEY Hogg, you've heard all my arguments against the existence of God.

HOGG Yes.

SHELLEY You agree with them?

HOGG Yes.

SHELLEY You don't disagree with them the tiniest little bit?

HOGG No.

SHELLEY You are not prepared to find the slightest flaw, the smallest mistake in my logic?

HOGG No.

SHELLEY Oh! I want an argument!

HOGG (*dry*) Try the Bishop.
(*Slight pause*)

23

SHELLEY What?

HOGG Nothing.

SHELLEY Hogg, let's go and call on the Bishop.

HOGG The Bishop of Oxford?

SHELLEY Yes.

HOGG (*dismissing it*) You're insane.

SHELLEY Somebody who knows all the arguments. Somebody who will really stand by God.

HOGG Bishops don't discuss theology with undergraduates.

SHELLEY Could the Bishop convert me? Hogg, could I convert the Bishop? How can I get the Bishop to argue?

HOGG (*dry*) Write him a letter. . . . Come on, let's go to my rooms and have some tea.

SHELLEY Suppose I got a pamphlet printed?

HOGG Eh?

SHELLEY Something official looking, serious . . . it would have to be unsigned.

HOGG In this university? I should think so.

SHELLEY No, it's not that. I wouldn't sign it because if he thinks the pamphlet is written by an undergraduate, he'll just dismiss it. I want him to take the arguments seriously. I want him to answer them as powerfully and logically as he can.

HOGG How can the Bishop reply if you don't sign?

SHELLEY I'll send a copy of the pamphlet, accompanied by a letter from a slightly bewildered gentleman. This gentleman has read the pamphlet and is confused and dazzled by the unanswerable splendour of its logic—his faith is shaken, crumbling—he needs help—he would be so grateful for his lordship's comments upon the pamphlet. I'll get someone to post it from an address in London . . . and I'll sign it . . . Jeremiah Stukeley.

HOGG Jeremiah Stukeley.

SHELLEY A respectable name. A churchwarden's name. The name of a grocer with philosophical inclinations. Who could resist answering a letter signed

Jeremiah Stukeley? Come! Let's get back to my rooms!

HOGG But what about. . . ?

SHELLEY Oh, come on! Come on! I want to get started!
(*They go*)

ACT ONE/SCENE TWO

A table, four chairs.
Enter SCOUT *showing in* WALKER, *a heavy pompous man.*

SCOUT This is the Master's room, would you be so kind as to wait here, Mr Walker sir? The Master said he will be here directly.

WALKER Oh——

SCOUT Yes, Mr Walker sir?

WALKER Is the Master of the college expecting anyone else?

SCOUT I believe he expects the Reverend Mr Coplestone, sir.

WALKER Coplestone?

SCOUT Mr Coplestone did ask if he might see the Master, sir.

WALKER Thank you, that will be all.

(*Exit* SCOUT)
(WALKER *alone, looks with considerable virtuous rage at the pamphlet he is carrying*)
'The Necessity of Atheism'!
(WALKER *business which shows (a) his righteous indignation; (b) his wish to get the effect of his indignation just right*)
(*Enter* MASTER, *a scholar, a weak, kindly man*)

WALKER Ah, Master.

MASTER Walker—Walker!

WALKER You have seen this—this. . . .

MASTER Yes, I have, oh yes.

WALKER Disgusting and blasphemous! How dare . . .

MASTER Walker, my dear fellow. Coplestone will be here in a moment, he demanded to see me.

WALKER Demanded?

MASTER He's probably heard about this—this——

WALKER Opportunity?

MASTER Outrage.

WALKER What has this to do with Coplestone? He is not
even a fellow of this college.

MASTER He wants opportunity to display his—his—he's
hoping for a bishopric.

WALKER Coplestone a Bishop?

MASTER I do hope he gets it. I must say I find him very,
er—very——

WALKER Insincere?

MASTER Determined. So I sent for you as you are the
wretched boy's tutor and because I hear it was you,
er. . . .

WALKER Ripped asunder the veil of blasphemy.

MASTER Eh? Oh, yes. Now tell me, er, quickly, how did you
discover the pamphlet?

WALKER Well, Master. I was proceeding down the High
Street.

MASTER Ah yes, down the High, yes.

WALKER And as is occasionally my custom I paused to gaze
in the window of Munday and Slattery, the
booksellers.

MASTER The booksellers.

WALKER The booksellers.

MASTER Oh my dear Walker, please don't repeat me.

WALKER (*rather confused and put off his stroke by the
interruption*) Oh, I'm sorry—I——

MASTER Coplestone will be here in a minute.

WALKER Oh yes, where was I?

MASTER In the High.

WALKER Outside Munday and Slattery. What was my
dismay to find that the windows of Munday and
Slattery were stuffed——

MASTER Stuffed?

WALKER Stuffed with copies of this. Everywhere the words,
'The Necessity of Atheism' dancing before my eyes.

MASTER Pretty metaphor.

WALKER When I had sufficiently collected myself. . . .

MASTER (*sympathetic and confirming*) Shock, shock.

27

WALKER I entered the establishment and demanded to know the meaning of this—this——

MASTER World?

WALKER Outrage. I inquired of the shopman—an assistant—he informed me that not ten minutes earlier Mr Shelley——

MASTER Ah!

WALKER That Mr Shelley had entered the shop, strewn the pamphlets on the counter and instructed they be sold for sixpence.

MASTER Sixpence? That seems rather a lot. (*Continuing through* WALKER'S *following lines*) Not very good quality paper either. Seven pages. . . . Indifferently printed. . . .

WALKER I thereupon demanded to see Mr Munday or Mr Slattery. Munday was not on the premises. I drew Slattery's attention to the obnoxious nature of the publication.

MASTER . . . works out at a penny a page. . . .

WALKER He was entirely ignorant of the whole affair. He was aghast.

MASTER Aghast?

WALKER In a flash he apprehended the extremely delicate nature of the situation in which he might find himself *vis-à-vis* the university authorities.

MASTER We buy all our books at Munday and Slattery.

WALKER There we buy all our books. With commendable promptitude, nay with precipitant haste, Slattery threw himself——

MASTER (*identifying and murmuring through line*) Threw—threw——

WALKER Threw himself upon the pamphlets and carried them to the back of the shop where they were burned in the kitchen fire.

MASTER Burned, eh?

WALKER Burned. 'The Necessity of Atheism' was burned in my presence.

MASTER Burned.

WALKER When I look upon—when I contemplate this ancient university, when I consider the long centuries of godly and scholarly instruction, the tablets of learning, the respected mentors, the revered preceptors. . . .

MASTER Burned in the back kitchen.

WALKER You will, of course, expel him.

MASTER Oh come, Walker, expulsion, do you really think that is quite necessary?

WALKER Necessary!

MASTER Surely a reprimand. . . .

WALKER Repri——? A puerile whipper-snapper, not yet twenty, questions the established dogmas of fifteen generations! Flouts his preceptors and his God with blasphemous, abominable, obscene—flogging is too good for him!

MASTER But you say all the copies were burned.

WALKER Indeed they were but——

MASTER Then won't it be much simpler to ignore the whole thing?

WALKER Simpler?

MASTER If we expel him we'll have to tell everybody why and all about it. So much talk and fuss.

WALKER I cannot let it go at this. It's not honest or godly.

MASTER And just at this moment I have such an interesting piece of research, no really, Walker.

WALKER It revolts me. I am revolted.

MASTER Quite right, very proper. I respect your principles —high-minded, incorruptible—a credit to the college. But you see we're all so busy at this moment.

WALKER I—I must resign.

MASTER Oh come, you are far too valuable a . . . um . . . er . . . preceptor to allow yourself to be upset by the, er, foolishness of a mere undergraduate. Far too valuable, far too valuable. You see, my dear Walker, I have known little upsets like this before and they always settle down, yes, a kind of silly

29

liveliness that young men experience, a lively young fellow, you'll see he'll settle down and it'll all be forgotten. He'll forget it himself, probably turn out quite well. Good family, eh? Family in politics? Well he'll probably do very well. You see my dear fellow, it's the lively ones that have the zest. The zest of youth, and when they settle down. . . . No, no, leave it to me. Eh? Yes?

WALKER Well if you think there is good in him. . . . I would not want to destroy the career of a young man who might yet serve. . . .

MASTER Good. Oh I'm glad we got that settled before Coplestone arrived. What with hoping for the bishopric he's at so much pains to display his clarity of mind, he makes me feel quite nervous. By the by, Walker, my dear fellow, I came across something the other day—completely fascinating—I'd much appreciate your opinion—domestic customs of the Siennese—seventh century—really most delightful. I have it here with me I believe. . . .
(*Enter* SCOUT *followed by* COPLESTONE *who holds a copy of the pamphlet*)

SCOUT Reverend Mr Coplestone, sir.

MASTER Ah, Coplestone, do come in.
(*Exit* SCOUT)

COPLESTONE Good morning, Master. (*A nod to* WALKER) Walker.

WALKER Coplestone.

MASTER Ah yes, the unfortunate er . . . I see you've already——

WALKER Where did you——

MASTER Mr Walker, *please*. Coplestone, we have decided, having the best interests of the university at heart, that no good purpose will be served by—we have decided to let the matter rest.

COPLESTONE Indeed.

MASTER Since all the copies were burned.

COPLESTONE Burned?

MASTER All the copies have been burned.

COPLESTONE They have?

MASTER Owing to Walker's presence of mind all the copies in Munday and Slattery have been——

WALKER Burned.

MASTER . . . so it seemed to me by far the best—er—I'm so sorry you bothered to come.

(*Slight pause*)

COPLESTONE And the other copies?

WALKER Other copies?

MASTER What other copies?

COPLESTONE The copies which were sent to all the professors, all the heads of colleges and the Bishop.

MASTER The Bishop!

COPLESTONE Probably to all the Bishops. He seems a dedicated young man.

MASTER Oh dear.

COPLESTONE Each pamphlet accompanied by a letter in your student's handwriting signed Jeremiah Stukeley.

MASTER Jeremiah——

WALKER But why should he not use his own name?

COPLESTONE He did not want to be found out.

MASTER I don't feel very well, I think I'll go and lie down.

COPLESTONE You had better stay here.

MASTER Oh.

(*Pause*)

What are we going to do.

COPLESTONE You must expel him.

WALKER Ah.

(COPLESTONE *rings a bell*)

MASTER Are you quite sure he wrote the note? The note signed Jeremiah—er——

(COPLESTONE *hands the* MASTER *a paper who passes it on to* WALKER)

WALKER That is his handwriting.

(*Enter* SCOUT)

COPLESTONE Please ask Mr—what's his name?

WALKER P. B. Shelley.

COPLESTONE Find Mr P. B. Shelley and bring him here at once. The Master of the college would like to see him. (*Exit* SCOUT)

MASTER (*hysterical*) Please, gentlemen, don't let's get hysterical.

COPLESTONE (*cold*) Who is hysterical? (*Pause*) What is your opinion of the pamphlet?

WALKER Have you actually read it?

COPLESTONE It is not without interest, or merit.

WALKER The drivelling of an undergraduate. No more worthy of serious consideration than if it had been written by a woman or a monkey.

COPLESTONE The style is immature, these undergraduates sometimes have an over-confidence which can be irritating; however, the argument——

WALKER Can you seriously——

COPLESTONE Oh yes, forceful, clear-headed, even brilliant—for so young a man. Potentially quite a powerful intellect.

MASTER Then why do you want to expel him?

COPLESTONE The world must be shown that we will not tolerate radicals in this university.

WALKER But this isn't your college——

MASTER Why should he tell me what to do?

COPLESTONE Because it is known that I have received a copy. I am thus compelled to show where I stand. . . . I agree with you, Master, that had you been able to stifle the matter, had all the copies indeed been burned, it would have been much wiser to ignore it. However—now when the young man arrives I suggest we are seated. Master you must sit in the middle.

MASTER But what am I going to say?

COPLESTONE You confront him with the pamphlet, then you expel him.

MASTER What if he denies writing it?

COPLESTONE We examine him.

WALKER We have his letter.

32

MASTER Suppose he denies he wrote that?

COPLESTONE (*to* WALKER) You can identify his writing?

WALKER I can. And there is always Slattery's shopman.

MASTER But he only told the shopman to sell the pamphlet, he didn't say he wrote it.

COPLESTONE Do you not see, Master, that so long as it is absolutely clear to everyone, that we have thoroughly examined this young man, then no one can say that we are failing in our moral duty. Suppose he does deny writing the pamphlet, we know he wrote it.

WALKER Of course we do.

COPLESTONE But if he is clever enough to convince us that he did not when we know that he did, then he is clever enough to convince everyone else. And our hands are clean.

WALKER He won't deny it.

MASTER No, he won't deny it, he seems a truthful boy.

WALKER Then we must write out a notice of expulsion and get the business over as soon as possible.

MASTER It seems so drastic, it could ruin a young man's life.

COPLESTONE It will ruin our lives if it becomes known that we condone his action.

WALKER Remember the Bishop.

MASTER The Bishop!

COPLESTONE Be firm.

(*Enter* SCOUT)

SCOUT Mr Shelley.

(*Enter* SHELLEY)

SHELLEY Good morning, Master, you asked to see me? Mr. Walker good morning. Good morning sir.

(*A tense pause while the* MASTER *nerves himself*)

MASTER (*almost inaudible*) Are you the author of this pamphlet?

SHELLEY I beg your pardon, sir?

MASTER Are you the author of this pamphlet?

WALKER This! Did you write it? 'The Necessity of Atheism'.

COPLESTONE Did you write this pamphlet?

WALKER Did you or did you not write this pamphlet?

MASTER Are you the author of this pamphlet?

SHELLEY From your manner, gentlemen, which if I may say
so, is very strange, it is quite clear that if I say yes
to your question you will punish me.

WALKER Did you write this pamphlet?

SHELLEY You have set up a court and by your manner have
already found me guilty. But I see here no
witnesses, no counsel. No agreed order by which
my interests may be protected and which may
preserve me from your naked malice. The meanest
criminal that ever drew breath is not convicted
without proper trial, nor sentenced save under a
recognized and public code of laws established and
maintained by statute. By what right then, I must
ask, do you set up this tribunal?

MASTER Er—I—er——

WALKER Now look here, young man——

SHELLEY (*still quietly, but enjoying the sensation of his mind
working clearly and his tongue finding the words, and
of outfacing these gentlemen*) I would ask again, sir,
I would know by what right this court is impanelled
in judgment against me. Under what statute am I
accused? By what code shall I be punished? Who
appointed you my judges? You set up a private
court quite outside the laws of the realm by which
we are governed and utterly out of their control.
This jumped-up tribunal, this court of inquisition,
this star chamber, is unworthy and illegal. We are
free men, sir, and this is a free country.

MASTER Oh.

WALKER How dare you bandy——

SHELLEY I hesitate not to affirm that the opinions contained
in the pamphlet coincide with my own; but were
they as false as the visions of a calvinist it would
still be the duty of those who love liberty and
virtue to raise their voice indignantly against such

34

persecution, against such coercive suppression of opinion which, if false, needs but the opposition of truth; which, if true, must ultimately prevail in spite of force.

WALKER Ah!

COPLESTONE Walker—keep your dignity. Master hold firm.

SHELLEY Again I demand: by what right do you assemble to judgment? What can be adduced in palliation of an outrage so insulting to humanity and justice? A university that presumptuously calls itself the sanctuary of freedom whilst it infringes every right of thought and speech. I conceive by the promise held out by your zeal, sir, that we may not despair of beholding once more the flames of persecution kindled at Smithfield!

WALKER Young man. You outrage every—how dare you shout at us like this about justice. We are your preceptors!

SHELLEY Old men! Old men! Fathers! Bishops! You set yourselves up and demand we obey! Never will I obey where I cannot respect.

WALKER (*gasping and flopping about*) Op—op—op——

MASTER (*feebly*) I—I——

COPLESTONE Did you write this pamphlet?

SHELLEY Never will I answer such a question so put in such circumstances.

(*Silence*)

(*The* MASTER *confers with* WALKER *and* COPLESTONE)

MASTER You are expelled.

(*Pause*)

SHELLEY Expelled.

(*Pause*)

May I ask for what reason?

COPLESTONE For contumaciously refusing to answer the question put to you.

(*Exit* SHELLEY)

(*Long silence while they recover.*

35

COPLESTONE That was unbelievable.

WALKER He should be flogged.

MASTER Yes, well, we expelled him.

COPLESTONE Ah well, this prompt action will demonstrate to important people that we won't tolerate radicals. But my goodness me, what an extraordinary young man, who is he?

MASTER Walker is his tutor, he can tell you.

WALKER Quite a stable background. His father is a member of Parliament.

COPLESTONE (*very quiet*) Well?

WALKER His grandfather is a baronet, Sir Bysshe Shelley.

MASTER That must be where he got his middle name Bysshe, unusual, don't you think.

COPLESTONE (*to* WALKER) Yes?

WALKER The boy is heir by entail, after his father, to a large fortune. Extremely wealthy family, considerable influence in the government, the boy was going into politics—the Duke of Norfolk looks on him as a protégé I believe.
(*Pause*)

COPLESTONE And you tell me this now.

WALKER Eh? But——

COPLESTONE But what?

WALKER You didn't ask me before. (*Pause*) We had to punish him.

COPLESTONE But not expel him.

WALKER I don't understand.

COPLESTONE It could have been smoothed over, treated as a boyish prank, some small punishment which showed we disapproved but did not take it seriously and now . . . now . . . you tell me he has the ear of the Duke of Norfolk.

MASTER Yes, His Grace will have considerable influence in the naming of Bishops.

COPLESTONE What did you say?

MASTER The Duke will er—nothing.

COPLESTONE It is not too late. We must get him to deny the

pamphlet and reinstate him.

WALKER What!

COPLESTONE If he denies it, we tell everyone we have made inquiries, our hands are clean.

WALKER But we know he did it—the note—Slattery's shopman.

COPLESTONE The shopman we need not examine officially. The note—can you swear—*on your life*—that is Shelley's writing?

WALKER I can.

COPLESTONE Master?

MASTER Eh? Er—well——

WALKER I must protest—I——

COPLESTONE Protest and be damned. An unofficial message to the boy himself will be best. Mind you, if he persists in his present attitude then I must protect myself—I mean we must protect the university.

WALKER But how?

MASTER (*shaking his head*) He will not agree. No, he will not agree.

COPLESTONE We shall have to make sure that his father and—er, other influential persons, receive a correct account of the business.

(*They go*)

ACT ONE/SCENE THREE

MISS FERNEY, *the teacher.*
HARRIET WESTBROOK, *aged 16.* HARRIET *is*
exquisitely pretty, one of those girls whose dress is
always fresh and whose hair is always clean.
MISS MEEKS, *a pupil.*
THE FIDDLER *who accompanies.*
A dancing class, HARRIET *and* MISS MEEKS *are*
dancing together.

FERNEY Are we ready, young ladies? I think the minuet this
morning, Mr Cawther. Three, four and—Dip step
dip step step step, etc., etc., et al. Very nice, young
ladies, keep it going. (*To Audience*) This is Miss
Fenning's Academy for Young Ladies; it stands on
the edge of Clapham Common, a most healthy
situation. I am Miss Ferney. (*To girls*) Good.
Good. . . . Keep your head *up*, Miss Meeks,
prettily! Observe Miss Westbrook, see how Miss
Westbrook holds her head. Dip step dip step step
step. Watch your hands, young ladies. Look at Miss
Westbook's hands. Very well, rest awhile, young
ladies. Don't flop, Miss Meeks.
Now remember, young ladies, the ballroom—is, er,
well is *important*, is it not? There is something—
liberating—about a lady who dances well, who, as
she moves, displays a graceful elastic figure and yet
nothing could be more proper in polite society. A
young lady may—display—her charms confident that
what she is doing is quite seemly. Dancing is indeed
a healthful artistic relaxation and an *opportunity*.
Now, Miss Westbrook, how have you progressed
with that little allemande we set you last week?
May we perhaps see?

(HARRIET *dances very well, simply and gracefully.*
She is so pretty it's a joy to look at her)
(MISS FERNEY *hovers, counting, expressing, etc.*)
Very pretty, I think you should work a little more
on the final section I——
(*Enter* MISS PYBUS, *a teacher. Followed by* HELLEN
SHELLEY *who is looking tearful and rebellious. She is
about fourteen*)

PYBUS Stand there in the corner, Hellen Shelley, until I
give you leave to come away. Oh, Miss Ferney, I
didn't know you were here.

FERNEY It's quite all right, Miss Pybus, we are just going.

PYBUS No one is to speak to Hellen Shelley, she is in
disgrace.

FERNEY That will be all, Mr Cawther.
(*Exit* FIDDLER)
You hear that, young ladies? Hellen Shelley is in
disgrace.

PYBUS (*semi-discreetly to* MISS FERNEY) She said that Miss
Thistlethwaite was a—fibber.

FERNEY A fibber!

PYBUS Worse than that.

FERNEY Worse!

PYBUS She used a different word.

FERNEY Oh dear me, oh goodness gracious.

PYBUS The brother—

FERNEY Hellen Shelley's brother?

PYBUS The brother who was expelled from Oxford
University.

FERNEY For——

PYBUS Precisely. Miss Thistlethwaite said that he will
burn in hell for ever.

FERNEY And this girl said Miss Thistlethwaite was a——?

PYBUS Just so.

FERNEY Run along, young ladies, and remember, no one is
to speak to Miss Shelley.
(HARRIET *and* MISS MEEKS *exit*)
She should have her mouth washed out with soap

and water.

PYBUS She should be whipped.

(FERNEY *and* PYBUS *exit*)

(HELLEN *is left crying*)

(*Re-enter* HARRIET)

HARRIET Your brother must be a terrible person.

HELLEN Oh! Oh!

HARRIET Truly terrible.

HELLEN Oh!

HARRIET He will burn in hell for ever, won't he?

HELLEN Oh!

HARRIET He must be so awful!

HELLEN No.

HARRIET So devilish!

HELLEN No.

HARRIET So wicked!

HELLEN He's not.

HARRIET What is it like to have a brother who——

HELLEN He's not wicked.

HARRIET But he must be, mustn't he?

HELLEN He's not—He's Bysshe—He's wonderful.

HARRIET Bysshe? Is that his name?

HELLEN Yes.

HARRIET Bysshe . . . Bysshe. . . .

HELLEN Father is so angry with him, he says he can't come
home, he won't have him home, and he won't send
him any money or anything until Bysshe apologizes
and says he believes in God.

HARRIET Estranged!

HELLEN Father has stopped his allowance.

HARRIET Disinherited!

HELLEN Oh, Father can't disinherit him.

HARRIET What?

HELLEN The money, it's all entailed to Bysshe.

HARRIET (*scornful*) Money!

HELLEN He hasn't got any at the moment all the same.

HARRIET Starving!

HELLEN Father says he shan't have a penny till he says he

40

believes in God.

HARRIET And will he?

HELLEN I don't think so.

HARRIET Apostate!

HELLEN All his letters are sent back unopened. He's not supposed even to write to us.

HARRIET Cast out! Ostracized!

HELLEN It's awful.

HARRIET Awful!

HELLEN He has no money, and nothing to eat and he's lodging in a poky little room in Poland Street.

HARRIET Horrible! Frightful! Wicked! Damned! . . . Poland Street?

HELLEN Do you know it?

HARRIET It's not very nice.

HELLEN Miss Westbrook—Harriet——

HARRIET Yes?

HELLEN You are a weekly boarder, aren't you? You go home for the weekend, and today is Friday.

HARRIET Yes.

HELLEN Could you—will you—take Bysshe a message from me?

HARRIET (*horror struck*) Wh-at?

HELLEN A message and my pocket money, what I've been saving—I've been saving, you see, to buy some water colours, a paint box, a nice one, eighteen and sixpence, will you take it to him for me?

HARRIET Me—take——

HELLEN Oh yes.

HARRIET But I couldn't.

HELLEN Oh please.

HARRIET I couldn't.

HELLEN Oh please, he needs it so badly.

HARRIET But he's terrible, he's wicked.

HELLEN No.

HARRIET He doesn't believe in God.

HELLEN But it's not like that! He's the sweetest, dearest——

HARRIET A pariah! An outcast! A wastrel!

41

HELLEN He's my brother! He's wonderful! He's——

HARRIET Disinherited!

HELLEN Divine!

HARRIET No, no, I couldn't. I couldn't possibly. I couldn't.
Never.

HELLEN Please.

HARRIET No, no, I couldn't. No.

HELLEN Oh, Harriet, please.

HARRIET Don't ask me.

HELLEN Oh. (*Disappointed, turning away*) Oh, very well.
(*Pause*)

HARRIET All right, I will.
(*Enter* MISS FERNEY)

FERNEY Miss Westbrook!
You are not to talk to Miss Shelley, she is in
disgrace. Your sister is here.

HARRIET Eliza?

FERNEY She has called to take you home. (*Turning to*
HELLEN) Hellen Shelley, you may rejoin your class.

HARRIET (*to* HELLEN) What number Poland Street?

FERNEY (*turning to* HARRIET) I beg your pardon?

HELLEN Fifteen.

ACT ONE/SCENE FOUR

Enter HOGG *reading a letter.*

HOGG 'Fifteen Poland Street, eighth of May, eighteen
eleven. This place is a little solitary, but as a person
cannot be quite alone when he has ever got himself
with him I get on pretty well. I have employed
myself in writing poetry, and as I go to bed at
8 o'clock time passes quicker than it otherwise
might.' Mmm. . . .
Pause)
(*He resumes reading*)
'Solitude is horrible, how inconsistent I am, at one
moment thinking I could so overcome Nature's law
as to exist in complete seclusion, at the next
moment shrinking from solitude and starting from
my own company as it were that of a fiend,
anything rather than a continued communion with
self.'
(HOGG *continues reading to himself*))
(*Pause*)
(*Exit* HOGG *reading*)

ACT ONE/ SCENE FIVE

A park bench.
Excited laugher off.
Enter OLD WESTBROOK. *A determined man. A long and successful commercial career has given him a veneer of merchant dignity. His power can still frighten his household, but he's beginning to relax and enjoy his retirement.*

WESTBROOK (*hardly raising his voice*) Eliza! Eliza! Lizzie!

ELIZA (*off*) Yes, Pa?

WESTBROOK Come over here by the water and talk to your father.
(ELIZA *enters not over willingly*)
(ELIZA *is twenty-eight years old. Her breeding is a little too high-pitched to be genuine—unlike* HARRIET *who was born later in her father's fortunes*)
My, my, ain't it nice here by the Serpentine. Is that Knightsbridge Church there through the trees?

ELIZA I do wish you wouldn't call me Lizzie in front of company Pa, it ain't genteel. We ain't at the coffee house now, you know, said good-bye to all that. You've made your money and now you're a gentleman. I do wish you'd try and not be common.

WESTBROOK Yes, you're a pair of real fine young ladies. A credit to your old Pa. A baronet's grandson, eh? A baronet's grandson walking out with my little girl.

ELIZA Not walking out, Pa. Just walking.

WESTBROOK Oh? I don't know, Eliza. Three weeks now since you and Harriet took that message from his little sister. And we've seen a good deal of him since then. You know, Eliza, that young man is lonely, misses all his nice friends at Oxford. No one to talk to. That young man likes his audience. Well, ha,

44

ha, chuck, chuck, chuck.

ELIZA (*disgusted*) Oh, Pa—Ducks.

WESTBROOK Not seen a duck in years—not a live 'un—never had the time.

ELIZA Nasty dirty things.

WESTBROOK Chuck, chuck.

ELIZA Are you feeding ducks?

WESTBROOK Of course I am not feeding them, it's a stone.

ELIZA A stone?

WESTBROOK Yes, have a bit of fun. How old are you, Eliza? Twenty-eight aren't you, my dear? Well, never mind. A real lady like you and my money, we'll find you a nice husband. Oh yes, and a good 'un. Chuck, chuck. Ha, ha, missed! Waddle away. Harriet is sixteen and Mr Shelley is nineteen. Well?

ELIZA I think you ought to know, Pa, that he's been saying some very funny things to Harriet.

WESTBROOK It ain't what a young man says, Eliza, it's what he does. Our Harriet knows what she's about although she looks so meek and pretty. A baronet's grandson . . . so he's got some funny ideas has he? Funny ideas. A man that's got eighty thousand pounds coming to him can afford a few ideas.

ELIZA Eighty thousand pounds!

WESTBROOK That's right. I been making a few inquiries.

ELIZA Oh Pa!

WESTBROOK Your old Pa, he's a careful old Pa. He's not green.

ELIZA Eighty thousand pounds!

WESTBROOK If only my old lady could see us now. What a pearl we have bred, what a flower! My, my, what prettiness does for a woman. Might even catch a baronet's grandson.

(*Both are awed by the thought*)

ELIZA Pa.

WESTBROOK What do you think, Eliza?

ELIZA Lady Shelley . . . don't it sound lovely?

WESTBROOK D'you think she might, Lizzie? D'you think? Old

45

Westbrook's grandson a baronet, old Westbrook
that kept a coffee house and don't even know who
his grandpa was.

ELIZA Hush, Pa, don't talk about that.

WESTBROOK Only to you, my dear.

ELIZA Lady Shelley.

WESTBROOK Lady Shelley.

ELIZA Wait till they hear in East Cheap, Pa, and you'll be
as good as an alderman.

WESTBROOK I know my dear, but don't tell anyone yet Lizzie.
Don't whisper a word, not till it's certain.

ELIZA I must just tell Aunt Alice Pa. She's seen them
together and she's always asking after Mr Shelley.

WESTBROOK Well, be careful, gently does it, gently does it. And
let him talk, Eliza, talk as much as he likes, and
anything more than talk—you get my meaning?
You keep a sharp look out and anything more than
talk—even so much as—you tell me about it and
we'll have him. By God we will. She shall have her
baronet.

ELIZA They're coming this way, Pa.

WESTBROOK We'll go round shall we my dear? Shall we go on
round?

(WESTBROOK *and* ELIZA *stroll on upstage and
eventually off*)

(*Enter* SHELLEY *and* HARRIET)

SHELLEY But you can't *make* yourself believe can you?

HARRIET No, no.

SHELLEY You must be convinced by proof, by the witness of
others, by the evidence of your senses, by logic. If
something is proved then you can believe.

HARRIET Yes.

SHELLEY This bench is wood, isn't it?

HARRIET Er, yes.

SHELLEY And the Serpentine here is water. You know it's
water because you have seen many watery things,
you can compare and so you can easily believe that
this is water.

46

HARRIET Yes.

SHELLEY But supposing I was to say that there were here, above our heads an entire tree, a tree made of toffee. A toffee tree, d'you see? Its branches are all toffee, it spreads right above our heads, it shuts out the sun, and all toffee. Can you see it?

HARRIET Er, no.

SHELLEY Can you touch it?

HARRIET (*unconsciously venturing forth a hand*) No. But——

SHELLEY Harriet, a toffee tree.

HARRIET No, of course not.

SHELLEY It isn't there.

HARRIET No.

SHELLEY No matter how much I say it's there, you know it isn't there.

HARRIET No. Yes. No.

SHELLEY Belief in God is exactly the same. If I say there's a tree made of toffee stretching above our heads you don't believe me because you can't see it, you can't touch it, moreover, it's against all experience and logic. Why then should you believe that there's an old man with a white beard up there who created you and who watches everything you do?

HARRIET (*covering her ears*) Oh.

SHELLEY What's the matter?

HARRIET I mustn't listen to you.

SHELLEY Why not?

HARRIET You might make me believe you.

SHELLEY But——

HARRIET No, no, don't say anything more, please. Mr Shelley, God does exist.

SHELLEY How do you know?

HARRIET He does.

SHELLEY Because people say he does?

HARRIET Yes, no. No, no, please don't say anything.
(*Pause*)

SHELLEY Harriet, you must learn to think things out for yourself. Everything you do and everything you

47

believe you should think about hard and deeply so that you know quite clearly why you are doing it, and why you believe in it. You see people often deceive themselves and they want to deceive you too. Your teachers at school would probably say that it's wrong for you to listen to me, they might scold you for listening, but that wouldn't make it wrong to listen, they won't give you the real reason. I expect they say you must be good.

HARRIET But one must be good, mustn't one?

SHELLEY Do they say what goodness is? Isn't their goodness a set of rules? A set of rules that governs every eventuality in life. If you obey the rules you're a good girl, if you don't you're naughty? . . . Oh, ducks! Aren't they beautiful! Look at the colours, blue and brown and——

(He takes bread from his pocket and starts throwing it to the ducks)

HARRIET Do you keep the bread in your pocket always, in case you see any ducks, or birds or. . . .

SHELLEY Oh, not for the ducks especially! Bread—and raisins, I eat lots of bread and raisins, you can buy them almost anywhere—and they're so cheap I more or less live on bread and raisins.

(Pause)

All the evil in the world stems from just accepting what other people say, and not questioning it—the institution of marriage——

HARRIET Marriage.

SHELLEY Oh, you couldn't think of a situation more studiously hostile to human happiness than marriage. It's so disgusting, it kills all delicate and honest feeling. Imagine being forever chained to someone you could no longer love. How it must feed the hatred between you. 'Forsaking all other'. Be selfish, cold, indifferent towards all other beings, live in your little world of festering fidelity. Women and men must live together in friendship:

48

free, equal and pure. Delicate impulses welling forth in primal simplicity. Chastity! The virtue of the cheaply virtuous. Purity! Is it pure to remain chaste so you can sell your chastity on the market to the highest bidder? Is it not truly pure to give yourself, delicately, freely, generously, in honour, to a man of honour?

There is a book I should like to lend you, an amazing, remarkable, truly beautiful book, by a woman, called the *Rights of Women*, have you heard of it?

(HARRIET *shakes her head*)

Calm, clear-headed, dignified, daring, oh a magical woman. Mary Wollstonecraft. Mary Wollstonecraft. Mary Wollstonecraft.

(*He is nearly prostrating himself so great is his reverence*)

She lived with a man, openly, and bore him a child. He left her—inevitably, of course, because one of them would very likely have left the other, naturally, in the course of time, since they were honest people. But because of the monstrous pressures of society, oh, I am convinced of this! Think of her pain, her loneliness, a temporary pain, like the pain of a widow perhaps, I mean she could have met someone else, could she not, who would have healed her pain? But when he left her, she was an outcast from society, society had cast her forth. She tried to drown herself . . . she tried to drown herself . . . but she lived, she lived and married William Godwin. The great Godwin, author of *Political Justice*. What a union of great and noble minds! Godwin, that is another author you must read. Mary Wollstonecraft and William Godwin. . . .

(*Pause*)

ELIZA (*off*) Harriet! Harriet! We are going home now, dear.

(*Enter* ELIZA *and old* WESTBROOK)

Will you not come home with us, Mr Shelley, and have a little supper?

(SHELLEY *signifies assent*)

Oh, dear, tomorrow is Monday. Back to school, my darling.

SHELLEY School?

ELIZA Harriet has to go back to school tomorrow, Mr Shelley.

SHELLEY Oh. . . . May I write to you at school, Harriet? We will talk by letter.

SHELLEY, *a book in his hand as usual, and several
more stuffed in his pockets.*
Enter HELLEN SHELLEY.

SHELLEY (*not raising his voice too much*) Hellen! Hellen!

HELLEN I couldn't get here any sooner, they kept me in
after class. I must be back by seven——
(SHELLEY *looks at his watch*)
What time is it? Suppose they see you.

SHELLEY Twenty to. We can see the windows.

HELLEN Of the school? Yes, yes we can. I can see Miss
Prosser.

SHELLEY We're too near. . . . You see that tree over there?
When I tell you, go over as quickly as you can, and
get behind it. But don't run, you'll attract
attention. (*He looks to see if it's clear*) Right.
(HELLEN *crosses,* SHELLEY *pauses then crosses after
her*)
Now.

HELLEN They sent for father.

SHELLEY What!

HELLEN Father came, it was awful. He said he had
disowned you, he'd no control over you, he was
livid.

SHELLEY What about Harriet?

HELLEN They say she's terrible because she says she agrees
with you.

SHELLEY Ah!

HELLEN No one will speak to her. No one's allowed to.

SHELLEY You do?
(HELLEN *nods,* SHELLEY *is pleased*)
Now tell me exactly what happened.

HELLEN Harriet was reading one of your letters in class.

SHELLEY Well?

51

HELLEN Miss Pybus saw her and confiscated the letter and read it, and——

SHELLEY Read it——?

HELLEN Yes.

SHELLEY She read a private letter!

HELLEN That's nothing, it's school. What do you expect?

SHELLEY She read a private letter! Reading private letters, punishing her simply because she has a mind of her own. Hellen, you must stand against this. You must get them all together, all the pupils, all your frinds and you must make them see——

HELLEN But——

SHELLEY You must make them understand, that if they put up with this, being treated as silly, unthinking children, they connive at their own degradation.

HELLEN But I can't do that, it's just a little school, I mean. . . .

SHELLEY You must stand against injustice wherever you find it. Hellen, dearest, you must see there's no difference between your little school and the whole world.

HELLEN But it's not like that, I can't . . . we're only . . . it's silly—how can I. . . ?

SHELLEY I did. It's just the same as Oxford, there's no justice or dignity in anything they do, they are utterly corrupt and you must stand against them or you, too, will be corrupted.

HELLEN Yes, but you—you're big and important, it's the big world, you're a man.

SHELLEY The school is your world, within the context of school the situation is exactly the same.

HELLEN But you're a man.

SHELLEY It's no different for women.

HELLEN It is.

SHELLEY It's degrading what women put up with.

HELLEN Degrading?

SHELLEY It degrades me as a man.

HELLEN I don't understand what you mean.

SHELLEY You're being silly.

HELLEN I'm not, I'm not.

SHELLEY Don't cry, you mustn't cry about serious things.

HELLEN I'm not crying, I can't help crying.

SHELLEY Be logical!

HELLEN Don't.

SHELLEY Don't say don't and don't cry. You must face up to it.

HELLEN I can't help it.

SHELLEY You must.

HELLEN I'm only a woman.

SHELLEY You're a human being.

HELLEN I'm not even a woman. I'm not grown up.

SHELLEY Oh, Hellen, dear, dear Hellen! How they have corrupted you! How they have weakened you! Well, dry your eyes, you've got to go, it's five to seven.

HELLEN You're being so hard.

SHELLEY I'm not, I'm being logical and there's nothing wrong with my logic.

HELLEN I know there isn't. But I can't.

SHELLEY (*made very tender by the confession*) Oh, Hellen.

HELLEN I'm sorry, I'm sorry.

(*He is comforting her*)

SHELLEY You've got to go. Wait, I'll see if it's safe.

HELLEN I nearly forgot, here. (*She gives him a little money*) I saved it from collection on Sunday, I put in a button instead.

(*They are both laughing and crying*)

SHELLEY Oh, Hellen.

HELLEN Oh, Bysshe.

SHELLEY Now, listen, listen carefully. Tell Harriet you've seen me, tell her to keep up her courage. Tell her I say she must go home, she must demand to go home. She must not allow herself to suffer this degradation and unhappiness. She must demand to go home. Right?

(*She nods, he checks it's safe for her to go, they give*

53

each other an affectionate kiss and she slips off)
(*Pause*)
We need women who dare! Women who dare. Oh, for a woman who would dare.
(*Exit* SHELLEY)

ACT ONE/SCENE SEVEN

Enter OLD WESTBROOK, ELIZA *and* TWO SERVANTS
who are struggling with a sofa.

WESTBROOK Put it there! Put it there! If she wants to lie down
in my house she can lie down here. Where is she?

1ST SERVANT Who, sir?

WESTBROOK Who, sir! Miss Harriet!

SERVANT She's downstairs, sir.

WESTBROOK Tell her I want her in up here, in the little sitting
room. And when Mr Shelley calls I want him
shown up here.

(*Exit* SERVANTS)

ELIZA You are going to let him see her.

WESTBROOK See her? I'm going to make him marry her.

ELIZA Please, Pa, don't shout.

WESTBROOK All my daughters are wilting around in heaps! I'll
horsewhip him. I'll not be made a fool of in front
of my friends. I'll take him to court.

ELIZA She says he has never promised her anything.

WESTBROOK Don't you speak to me like that.

ELIZA Please, Pa, try not to shout, Harriet is very poorly.

WESTBROOK Poorly my foot. (*Mimicking*) No one'll talk to us at
school, so we all get upset. So she makes herself ill,
shams poorly and has herself sent home. I tell you
either she gets herself promised to that young man
or back she goes to school. How long's it going to
be before this gets to the aldermen? And your
Aunt Alice blathering. Oh my God! Three days
and it'll be rife through East Cheap! Wait till they
hear I got a daughter that's an atheist. Old
Westbrook's girl an atheist! An atheist! God strike
me! You send 'em to a nice school. . . .

(HARRIET *enters during this and* WESTBROOK
includes her in his diatribe)

55

... class and expense, to get a bit of polish what you and your old lady never had, make some nice friends. And she has to meet up with an atheist. A damned blue-blooded atheist. A damnable blue-blooded atheist with a sense of honour!

ELIZA Mr Shelley is a gentleman.

WESTBROOK A gentleman would've had her by now the way she's been carrying on.

ELIZA Pa!

WESTBROOK You shut up. (*To* HARRIET) Tell me, girl: has there been any—has there been the least hint of—have we got anything on him?

HARRIET What father?

WESTBROOK Any *meddling*?

ELIZA Certainly not.

WESTBROOK Blast the girl! An atheist and nothing to show for it. What's going on? He's normal ain't he? Any other house a young chap calls every day and you know what he's about. But all this one does is chat about the Poor Law in Ireland and Political Muckabout.

ELIZA *Political Justice.*

WESTBROOK Eh?

ELIZA *Political Justice,* Pa, by William Godwin.

WESTBROOK Got you on it too, has he?

ELIZA I am generally here when Mr Shelley calls.

WESTBROOK Ah hah!

ELIZA Eh?

WESTBROOK So that's it.

ELIZA What's what?

WESTBROOK Now look here. A bit less of the chaperone, if you please, not so much hanging around.

ELIZA (*the thought beginning to dawn*) The decencies must be observed . . . must they not?

WESTBROOK Decency my foot! Decency don't get a girl wed. You get my point? . . . Now look here, Harriet. You understand me? I mean what I say. Do you hear me?

56

HARRIET Yes, father.

WESTBROOK I am not going to be made a fool of in front of my friends. I've worked hard for the respect I've got and I'm going to keep it. You are going to marry this young man.

HARRIET I can't make him marry me. He's done me no harm. Made me no promises.

WESTBROOK Shall I spell it out?

HARRIET I can't make him marry me. I wouldn't make him if I could.

WESTBROOK Then back you go to school tomorrow, and there you stay.

HARRIET I won't! I won't go back to school!
(*Bell rings downstairs*)

ELIZA That's him, Pa.

HARRIET I won't go back to school.

WESTBROOK (*sneering*) Then where will you go? Out on the streets? For I will not have an atheist here in my house.

ELIZA For heaven's sake, Pa, you're in no state to see Mr Shelley now.

WESTBROOK No state to be polite to him.
(*Exit* WESTBROOK)

ELIZA Harriet! Throw yourself on him, make him get you in the family way.

HARRIET Eliza!

ELIZA Pa will force him to marry you.

HARRIET What wickedness. I'd rather die. I'd rather kill myself.

ELIZA You'd commit suicide if he doesn't marry you? Tell him that.

HARRIET You mean if I say I'll kill myself. . . .

ELIZA He'd give away his shirt, his very shoes, if someone asked. . . .
(SERVANT *shows in* SHELLEY)
Oh, good evening, Mr Shelley.

SHELLEY Good evening, Miss Westbrook—Harriet. How are you, Harriet? Are you all right?

57

ELIZA We are indeed a little pale, but we'll be so much better now you are here. Will we not, Harriet. See! See!

SHELLEY Eh?

ELIZA Her eye it brightens! Her blood it kindles!

HARRIET Eliza!

SHELLEY You've been crying.

ELIZA (*an agony of archness*) L'amour! L'amour!

SHELLEY I beg your pardon?

ELIZA L'amour. (*Clutching her bosom*) Oh!

HARRIET (*clutching her head*) Oh!

ELIZA Harriet, my darling, what's the matter?

HARRIET My head.

ELIZA It's aching? Oh, my poor pet. Mr Shelley, her head is aching.

SHELLEY I'm afraid I've called at a bad time, perhaps it would be better if I. . . .

HARRIET Oh, no, no.

ELIZA No, no, no, no.

HARRIET Eliza dear, I know what would help my head. Some of your lovely green tea. Will you make me some, my dear? *Yourself.*

ELIZA Of course, my dear.

HARRIET Thank you, my love.

ELIZA Will you excuse me, Mr Shelley?

SHELLEY Of course, Miss Westbrook.

(*Exit* ELIZA)

SHELLEY Now tell me.

HARRIET He says I must go back to school.

SHELLEY But it's making you ill. You can't go.

HARRIET He says I must.

SHELLEY Tyrant.

HARRIET What shall I do?

SHELLEY Do? Resist him!

HARRIET My father?

SHELLEY That gives him no right to dictate to you, to cruelly force you to a degrading act.

HARRIET But what else can I do?

58

SHELLEY If he is unjust and tyrannical you must resist him.

HARRIET But how?

SHELLEY Just as you resisted your teachers you must resist him. If you submit you strengthen the hand of oppression and injustice. If you give in you are betraying the higher values of mankind. You mustn't weaken.

HARRIET Yes, er, no.

SHELLEY You do see?

HARRIET I know you are right.

SHELLEY Yes.

HARRIET You must be right. You're always right.

SHELLEY You mustn't just accept it because I say so.

HARRIET No.

SHELLEY You must think it out for yourself.

HARRIET Yes. I must resist him because he's being cruel and unjust.

SHELLEY That's right.

HARRIET Yes.

SHELLEY It's tyrannical.

HARRIET It's degrading.

SHELLEY It's cruel.

HARRIET But how can I stand against him?

SHELLEY How?

HARRIET Yes.

SHELLEY I stood against my father's injustice, you must do the same.

HARRIET But I haven't any money. I've nothing to live on, how can I live?

SHELLEY I live.

HARRIET But you're a man.

SHELLEY Man, woman, it makes no difference.

HARRIET It does.

SHELLEY It doesn't.

HARRIET It does.

SHELLEY (*being reasonable*) How? Tell me?
(*Slight pause.* HARRIET *feels she may be uttering an obscenity*)

59

HARRIET What would people say?
(*Slight pause*)

SHELLEY The good people, the really honourable people whom we value and respect. . . .

HARRIET But there aren't very many of them, are there?

SHELLEY But soon there will be thousands.

HARRIET But how many honourable people do you actually know?

SHELLEY I suppose . . . about five, but soon there will be hundreds—it only needs a few brave women—like Mary Wollstonecraft——

HARRIET The one who tried to drown herself? (*Pause*) I think Society is still a bit like that even now. You know I heard before she went into the water she tried to tie her skirt round her ankles. To prevent her skirt floating up you know . . . when she was dead. . . . If I have to leave this house where will I go? How will I live? If only they'd teach girls something useful, instead of deportment and a little French and the use of the globes. I see, I see it's a deliberate act to keep us inferior and helpless like you say. I see that. But you see it has *happened* to me, I can do nothing. If you—if some ordinary person, not noble or anything, heard of me, heard I'd left home, no money, nowhere to go, what would he think? What would they say? How would they treat me? They'd say I was—they'd say I was a. . . .

SHELLEY (*gently*) Don't say it.

HARRIET I'm not even fit to be a governess. If I was to leave this house, it would indeed be that—or dying of cold and starvation. I see what I could do. I must stand up for the dignity of women, I see that. I must resist him. Well, if I resist him he will turn me out of the house. That means a choice between going on the streets or . . . suicide.

SHELLEY Harriet.

HARRIET What else is there?

SHELLEY No.

HARRIET It's quite clear.

SHELLEY Wait, let me think. . . . I meet a girl who is kind
and friendly to me in my loneliness, and brings me
comfort when no one else will speak to me. I talk
to her freely—all the deep, but dangerous thoughts
that rise in my mind. It's not wrong to speak the
truth, indeed one has a duty to speak the truth—
but one must be ready to stand by one's word. And
sure enough she does encounter cruelty and
ill-usage. I tell her to resist and she does resist. She
cannot remain at home, her education has unfitted
her to earn her own living . . . and I am
responsible . . . I am responsible. . . . Harriet,
dearest, I must be your protector.

HARRIET What?

SHELLEY I must be your protector and help you, yes!

HARRIET Protector?

SHELLEY My opinions, my letters, you are in this position
because you have absorbed so freely, so readily, the
great principles that I have propounded. I am
responsible, I must protect you.

HARRIET But how? I mean. . . .

SHELLEY I shall be your dearest, most faithful, sincerest
friend.

HARRIET Oh.

SHELLEY I haven't very much money I'm afraid, but we shall
manage. We shall live together in delicate, affectionate
purity. Secure in our virtue and our friendship you
shall be a torch to the world, a paragon amongst
women. My friends shall be your friends. We shall
scorn the rest of the world even while we are an
example to them. Yes? Do you agree?

HARRIET What if you. . . .

SHELLEY Well?

HARRIET What if you should grow tired of me?

SHELLEY Tired? Tired of the sacred bond of friendship?

HARRIET What if you should change?

61

SHELLEY Passion may change yes, love indeed, mere love
may fade. But friendship, pure, reasonable,
disinterested friendship, is a bond for ever.

HARRIET You may have other friends.

SHELLEY Of course, and you also.

HARRIET No.

SHELLEY But you will.

HARRIET Never in the way you mean, *I* mean.

SHELLEY But, Harriet, do not confuse love and friendship.
Love indeed is selfish, exclusive, coldly indifferent
to the fate of all others, narrowly chaste.

HARRIET Yes.

SHELLEY That is love. Love is like that, not friendship.

HARRIET Yes, no.

SHELLEY It may seem difficult to understand at first.

HARRIET Yes.

SHELLEY But soon thousands will acknowledge your courage,
your nobility, your true virtue. We shall go through
life as affectionate companions, irrevocably bound
to each other by the sacred ties of friendship. No
chains of chilling legality, no lawyer's arrogant
coercion shall mar our beautiful relationship.
Together with other sincere and elevated beings we
shall celebrate life and ennoble mankind. Oh
Harriet! . . . You don't seem very moved.

HARRIET (*not moved*) Oh yes, I am, I am terribly but. . . .

SHELLEY Well?

HARRIET Mr Shelley, I couldn't live with you. I couldn't.

SHELLEY But why not?

HARRIET I don't know why.

SHELLEY But if it's a logical course of behaviour. . . .

HARRIET I know I'm being stupid and unworthy. . . .

SHELLEY But if you know it's right. You do believe it would
be right?

HARRIET I do, I do believe it would be right.

SHELLEY Well?

HARRIET I can't. . . . I suppose I'm just a coward.

SHELLEY You aren't.

HARRIET I must be.

> (*Long pause*)
> Mr Shelley . . . (*Pause*) There's something I ought to tell you.

SHELLEY Tell me.

HARRIET Oh. . . .

SHELLEY (*gently*) What is it? Tell me. (*Pause*) Please tell me.

HARRIET You'll despise me.

SHELLEY Despise you?

HARRIET Oh, I can't tell you.

SHELLEY I will never despise you.

HARRIET You will.

SHELLEY Harriet, please tell me what is on your mind. To share hardship, grief, trouble is the sacred right of friendship.

HARRIET Oh I'm so weak and silly.

> (*He tries to take her hand but she won't let him*)
> (*They sit silent*)

SHELLEY Please let me help you. I am your friend.

HARRIET (*almost inaudible*) I am not your friend.

> (*Pause*)

SHELLEY Dear Harriet, tell me what you mean.

> (*Pause*)

HARRIET Well, you know how you say that friendship is so much more noble than . . . than . . . love, and it's true . . . well . . . you . . . you see . . . I think that . . . I love you.

> (*Long pause*)
> Please, please don't touch me.
> (*Long pause*)

SHELLEY Harriet, dearest, will you marry me?

HARRIET Oh, I can't.

SHELLEY Why can't you?

HARRIET You don't believe in marriage, it's against your principles.

SHELLEY People are more important than principles.

HARRIET I can't marry you.

SHELLEY You must marry me.

63

HARRIET You don't believe in it.

SHELLEY I know I don't, but we must get married. You *must* marry me.

HARRIET I won't.

SHELLEY You shall.

HARRIET I shan't.

SHELLEY You must.

HARRIET I can't make you do what you think is wrong.

SHELLEY You cannot face this alone and I am responsible.

HARRIET It's blackmail.

SHELLEY It's friendship.

HARRIET Oh, Mr Shelley! Oh, Bysshe!

SHELLEY Harriet, dearest! Dearest Harriet, will you marry me?

HARRIET Very well then, yes, perhaps, if you are quite, quite sure.

(*Pause, he kisses her shyly*)

SHELLEY What pretty hands you have, I never noticed, so very, very. . . .

(*A more intense kiss*)

(*End of Act One*)

ACT TWO/SCENE ONE

Enter HARRIET *with the baby* IANTHE *in her arms.*

HARRIET Is it Ianthe then? Is it Ianthe? Yes! Yes! Yes! An
Ianthe. Papa will be home soon. Papa will be home.
Oh, Ianthe what a smile. What a smile. And Aunt
Eliza, her dear Aunt Eliza has come to stay with us.
Yes. I' sent it a lucky Ianthe? Ooh! You mustn't
put your tongue out. Dear Aunt Eliza I expect
she'll stay with us a long time. Won't that be nice?
Ianthe no! That's not lady-like, that's not ladylike
at all.
(*Enter* ELIZA)

ELIZA Harriet dear, here you are in the sitting-room? The
sitting-room! Such a nice view of the backyard.
Why is it that the furniture in lodgings is always so
hard? I must say two years married, two years
married and still living in lodgings. But they're quite
clean.

HARRIET You know very well, dear Eliza, that Bysshe thinks
luxury is wicked.

ELIZA How you manage on four hundred a year . . . four
hundred a year!—And half of that he gives away
to the poor. I expect you'll find it a bit difficult
now you've got Ianthe.

HARRIET I'm sure we'll manage.

ELIZA I'm sure you will. . . . But you must think of
Ianthe mustn't you? Charity begins at home. Tchk,
tchk. (*Enticing noise for baby*) Come to me my little
angel, come to your Aunt Eliza . . . tchk, tchk,
tchk. . . . What are you doing my love, copying?

HARRIET I like copying for Bysshe. It's very interesting.

ELIZA What's this?

HARRIET A pamphlet: the 'Declaration of the Rights of Man'

ELIZA (*reading*) 'Man has no right to kill his brother. It is

no excuse that he does so in uniform, he only adds
the infamy of servitude to the crime of murder.'
Well. . . .

(*Pause*)

He wants to change the world with his pamphlets,
doesn't he?

HARRIET He wants to make the world a better place.

ELIZA So we have Injustice in Ireland, and the Wickedness
of Judges and Marriage——

HARRIET And God.

ELIZA That's right dear. All to make the world a better
place. . . . Humph. . . .

HARRIET What do you mean: humph?

ELIZA Just humph.

HARRIET Eliza, what do you mean?

ELIZA For heaven's sake, Harriet, what good do they do?
Who reads them?

HARRIET Who reads them! Lots of people read them.

ELIZA Tell me.

HARRIET Lots of people . . . well a few. . . .

ELIZA Who?

HARRIET Mr Godwin reads them.

ELIZA Mr Godwin.

HARRIET He thinks Bysshe is wonderful.

ELIZA He would.

(*Pause*)

HARRIET Eliza, don't you like Mr Godwin?

ELIZA Oh those evenings at the Godwin's.

HARRIET Sometimes they do seem a little long.

ELIZA Talk, talk, talk. And to be quite honest I think Mr
Godwin is a bit common.

HARRIET Common?

ELIZA Have you noticed their teapot? Chipped. And those
covers, such nasty cheap stuff.

HARRIET But we haven't much money either. Bysshe says the
true nobility is nobility of mind.

ELIZA Bysshe can say that sort of thing because of the title
and the family money. It's a pity he doesn't get

hold of some of that money instead of wasting his time and energy on pamphlets. Make the world a better place! The world would be a sight better place for you with a bit of cash.

HARRIET (*reproving*) Eliza. . . .

ELIZA A woman in your position: the wife of the heir of the heir of a baronet, you should be in Society, you should be going to balls, giving soirées, dancing——

HARRIET (*enthralled by the idea*) Oh, Eliza!

ELIZA You could be having a fine time. And you ought to have a carriage. A lady in your position, and no carriage! And Ianthe shall marry an earl shall she not? An early-pearl, an earl.

HARRIET I think she's going to cry.

ELIZA No she's not.

HARRIET Perhaps you'd better giver her to me.

ELIZA She must *learn* to be happy.

(*Pause*)

HARRIET She's whimpering. Do let me hold her.

(*Pause*)

ELIZA I think she's hungry.

HARRIET Oh.

ELIZA She needs to be fed. (*Slight pause*) You must feed her.

HARRIET Oh.

ELIZA Now, Harriet, don't be silly.

HARRIET Do you really think——

ELIZA You know what I said. You're wearing yourself out.

HARRIET I'm sure Bysshe won't like it.

ELIZA He won't know.

HARRIET He'll find out.

ELIZA Hurry up before he gets back.

HARRIET He'll hate it. He'll say it's wrong.

ELIZA It's not Bysshe that's wearing himself out, going into a decline.

HARRIET I'm not in a decline.

ELIZA You're much paler than you were. You'll lose all your looks, then where will you be?

HARRIET If you really think——

ELIZA Yes I do.

HARRIET All right.

> (*Exit* HARRIET)
>
> (*Pause*)
>
> (*Enter* SHELLEY)

SHELLEY Harriet, dearest, is Ianthe with you?—Oh. . . .

ELIZA Good afternoon.

SHELLEY Good afternoon.

> (*Pause*)
>
> May I hold Ianthe?

ELIZA She's quite happy where she is.

SHELLEY I would very much like to hold my daughter. If you don't mind.

ELIZA It's not convenient.

SHELLEY Not convenient?

ELIZA Harriet is going to feed her.

> (*Pause*)
>
> (*to audience*) He can't stand me holding her.

SHELLEY (*to audience*) Ianthe is my darling child, and it's all that I can do to control myself when that woman is holding her.

> (*Enter* HARRIET *with a feeding-bottle. When she sees* SHELLEY *her first impulse is to hide it*)

HARRIET Oh. . . .

ELIZA Come on. Don't bother about him.

SHELLEY What? What do you mean? You're going to——

HARRIET Bysshe, dear, I don't think I——

ELIZA Oh for heaven's sake. What nonsense, here give it to me.

> (ELIZA *takes bottle and starts feeding* IANTHE)

SHELLEY What?—What!—Harriet! Harriet! Are you sick? Are you not well?

HARRIET I'm—I'm—it's all right.

SHELLEY Then why are you feeding Ianthe with a bottle?

HARRIET Oh——

SHELLEY Why aren't you feeding her yourself?

ELIZA It's bad for her.

68

SHELLEY Bad for you?

ELIZA Breast feeding is bad for the figure.

SHELLEY Bad for——!

ELIZA No lady suckles her own child.

HARRIET I'm sure Eliza knows best, she knows all about these things.

SHELLEY Harriet, please, please listen to me. We talked about this, we agreed. We agreed that since Nature gave a mother milk to feed her child there must be some good, some special reason, didn't we? Harriet, we agreed. You don't know what harm you may be doing. You don't know what you're doing. How can this give her what you can give her?

ELIZA Oh fiddle de dee.

SHELLEY This is cow's milk, Ianthe's not a calf.

ELIZA Tantrums!

SHELLEY Feed her! Feed her yourself!

HARRIET Everybody does it, please, Bysshe, don't make such a fuss.

SHELLEY Then everybody is wrong, cruelly wrong.

HARRIET It's just till we get a wet nurse.

SHELLEY We already have a nursemaid, we can't afford a wet nurse.

ELIZA It's bad for Harriet's nerves.

SHELLEY (*shouting*) What about Ianthe's nerves?

HARRIET She'll have to have a bottle for I shan't feed her.

SHELLEY You are stealing life and health from your own child.

HARRIET I'm not going to feed her.

ELIZA It's not ladylike.

SHELLEY Harriet! Harriet, I implore you!

HARRIET No.

ELIZA It's indelicate.

SHELLEY Oh God, oh my God. (*He tears open his shirt*) Why aren't I a woman? Give her to me! Ianthe! Drink! Drink! Here! Oh. . . . Oh. . . . Oh. . . . my God . . . my God. . . .

ELIZA Lawks a mercy. What a fuss. What a carry on!

HARRIET Bysshe! Bysshe. (*Scared*) Stop it. Oh stop him, stop him!

(*After a while* SHELLEY *calms down and* HARRIET *takes* IANTHE *from him*)

ELIZA It's very bad for Harriet. You are being extremely selfish.

(*Pause.* ELIZA *hands* HARRIET *the bottle and she feeds* IANTHE. *Pause. Exit* SHELLEY)

ACT TWO/SCENE TWO

Enter SHELLEY.

Enter HOGG.

HOGG Why, hello!

SHELLEY Oh, Hogg.

HOGG Fancy meeting you. It must be months since I saw
you. I've just been to the Inns of Court. You're
going this way?

SHELLEY I'm going to Godwin's bookshop.

HOGG Godwin's bookshop? William Godwin, you know
him? I'd very much like to meet him, may I come
too? Will you introduce me?

SHELLEY (*unenthusiastic*) By all means.

(*Pause*)

HOGG Well, shall we go?

SHELLEY If you like. (*Pause*) Well, I must bid you good-bye.

HOGG But——

SHELLEY Good-bye, my dear fellow, good-bye.

HOGG But you were going to take me to Godwin.

SHELLEY Oh yes, very well, if you wish.

(*Pause*)

HOGG How are Harriet and Ianthe?

SHELLEY Ianthe is well, very well, a delight.

HOGG And Harriet?

SHELLEY Ianthe is in Bath with her mother. I haven't seen
them this two months.

HOGG Oh—I see. . . .

(*Pause*)

SHELLEY Hogg, all is not well with Harriet and me.

HOGG I'm sorry.

SHELLEY Anyone who knows me must know that the
partner of my life must be one who can feel poetry
and understand philosophy, Harriet is a noble
animal but she can do neither. You know my ideals,

Hogg, my philosophy, the sacrifices I've—How can it demand otherwise than a woman of consummate courage, nobility and strength, and above all, education. That is the key. The power to reason, to understand, that makes her free to act. Educated as a man, to think as clearly and boldly as the best of men. With such a woman—with such a woman I could go on.

(*Pause.* SHELLEY *takes a phial from his pocket*)

HOGG Are you all right? Why, this is laudanum.

(*Pause*)

SHELLEY What is virtue? Can it be idiocy to cling to—Can urging to goodness become meaningless madness? What if ideals are betrayed? It is my duty—truly is it my duty to care for Harriet? Is duty a mockery?

(*Pause*)

HOGG Isn't this Godwin's shop. Perhaps we'd better go in.

(*They go in. Enter* SERVANT)

SERVANT Good morning Mr Shelley sir—Why——

HOGG Will you tell Mr Godwin that Mr Shelley would like to see him?

SERVANT Certainly, sir, but I'm not sure Mr Godwin is at home.

(*Exit* SERVANT)

(*Pause*)

HOGG Are you all right?

SHELLEY Yes, yes, I'm all right now.

HOGG So this is Godwin's bookshop . . . the great Godwin.

(*Pause*)

SHELLEY Where is Godwin? (*Pause*) Where can he be? (*Pause*) Why does Godwin not come?

(*Pause*)

(*Enter* MARY)

MARY Mr Shelley.

(MARY *draws back as she sees* HOGG)

SHELLEY Mary!

(SHELLEY *and* MARY *talk upstage. Exit* MARY)

72

SHELLEY Godwin is not at home, there is no point in our
staying.

HOGG Oh.

(*They go*)

Who was that? A daughter?

SHELLEY Yes.

HOGG A daughter of William Godwin.

SHELLEY A daughter of William Godwin and Mary
Wollstonecraft.

(*They exit*)

73

ACT TWO/SCENE THREE

Enter MARY, *about sixteen, smallish, almost mousy, quite pretty. Immensely intelligent. Quite sure of herself, even imperious. Like* SHELLEY *she carries a book.*

Enter CLARE, *the same age, vivacious with a great sense of adventure, very pretty in a dark, roguish way.*

Enter SHELLEY.

CLARE Mary, I'm so hot—Mary! Walking all the way from Holborn to St Pancras churchyard on a day like this. It's too much . . . whew! Which is your mother's grave?

MARY Well, Clare, you shouldn't wear such silly shoes.

CLARE I like pretty shoes.

MARY There's the church why don't you go and look?

CLARE Oh! Isn't it old!

(*Exit* CLARE)

MARY I hope you didn't mind walking.

(SHELLEY *looks miserable*)

Was it too hot for you?

(*He shakes his head*)

I hope my sister doesn't worry you, I'm afraid she chatters rather a lot. . . .

(*Pause*)

This is my mother's grave——

(*Re-enter* CLARE)

CLARE The church is so old that bits are falling off it. It's rather nice here. . . . Mary's mother's buried here somewhere, at least that's what we're supposed to have come all this way for. Did you ever hear how Godwin came to marry *my* mother, the present Mrs Godwin? Mary's mother, the first Mrs Godwin, died when Mary was born, isn't that sad and romantic? And papa was left with this orphan

74

and—isn't that a pretty flower? I wonder what it's
called? He asked lots of ladies to have him but they
were too sensible.

MARY Clare.

CLARE Godwin just wants to work, he can't be bothered
with us. Well, mama had lodgings near his. One
day she saw Pa through her window and she
leaned out and said, 'Is it possible I behold the
immortal Godwin?' So they got married. We
moved into Godwin's house. I got a father, Father
got a housekeeper, Mary got a sister, well, a sort of
sister; we're just about the same age, I'm a bit
older, I'm nearly seventeen. You look a bit glum.
Are you all right? Is it the heat? You do look
funny.

MARY Clare.

CLARE Well, he does, he looks very odd.

MARY Clare.

CLARE Mm?

MARY Mr Shelley and I are going to talk philosophy.

CLARE What?

MARY You won't like it, and you won't understand so
why don't you go and have a look inside the church.

CLARE I've already seen the church.

MARY Well, we're going to talk philosophy.

CLARE Oh. . . . Oh look! A butterfly!

(CLARE *follows the erratic course of the butterfly*
trying to catch it and exits)
(*Pause*)

MARY This is where my mother is buried, this is her
grave. (*Pause*) 'Mary Wollstonecraft Godwin.
Author of A Vindication of the Rights of Women.
Born 27th April 1757 died 10th September 1797.'
(*Pause*) This place is sacred to me.
(*Pause*)
Shelley, will you tell me something: You say in
'Queen Mab', in 'Queen Mab' you say:
'Woman and man, in confidence and love,

75

Equal and free and pure together trod'
If they are equal surely they've an equal right to. . . .
And you say:
'Then that sweet bondage, which is Freedom's self'
—and you mean love, do you not?
'Then, that sweet bondage, which is Freedom's self,
And rivets with sensation's softest tie
The kindred sympathies of human souls,
Needed no fetters of tyrannic law:'—that is:
needed no marriage.
'Those delicate and timid impulses
In Nature's primal modesty arose,
And with undoubted confidence disclosed
The growing longings of its dawning love,
Unchecked by dull and selfish chastity,
That virtue of the cheaply virtuous.'
You are married, a married man. Well, I know
your views upon love and marriage—that they
should not be selfish and exclusive and everything.
They're my mother's views . . . and my views and
. . . Well, being married, if you were to meet
someone whom you—liked and who liked—perhaps
more than liked—you. You—would you not feel—
being married and so unable to ask her to marry
you—I mean if you were to tell someone that you
loved her, because you were married you couldn't
ask her to marry you, could you? So if you said
you loved her and wanted her to love you, and
maybe she does, did love you—it would be like
asking her to—you are so fine and unselfish and
thoughtful, you would think you had no right to—
ask so much. And, I—I understand, because it is a
lot, these days, it won't always be like this, but it is
a lot now for a woman to—to . . . come to a man
without being married to him. . . . So it seems to
me, that it is so much that it should be the woman
who offers, don't you think? I mean if she really—
if she really. . . .

(He is filled with a radiance which he seeks to restrain lest it frighten her, it becomes a miraculous gentleness and warmth)
(He kisses her very gently)
(Very long pause)
(He reels from her embrace almost fainting)

MARY Shelley. . . . Are you all right?

SHELLEY 'The lightning is his slave; heaven's utmost deep
Gives up her stars, and like a flock of sheep
They pass before his eye, are numbered, and roll
on!
The tempest is his steed, he strides the air;
And the abyss shouts from her depth laid bare,
Heaven, hast thou secrets? Man unveils me; I have
none.'

(Blackout)

ACT TWO/SCENE FOUR

SHELLEY *and* MARY

SHELLEY Mary, darling, darling, dearest Mary. We mustn't tell your father.

MARY No?

SHELLEY I'm arranging a further loan for him.

MARY Another loan for father?

SHELLEY Yes.

MARY As well as the five hundred?

SHELLEY I'm borrowing against my inheritance. Oh! What joy to aid philosophy! Godwin himself puts it so well, he says: 'I am bound to employ my talents, my understanding, my strength, my time, for the production of the greatest quantity of the general good. I have no right to dispose of a shilling of my property at the suggestion of my own caprice.'

MARY Papa hasn't got very much property.

SHELLEY So you see we mustn't tell him yet, not until the loan is arranged, otherwise he might refuse—he is so fine—he might feel himself in a difficult position —accepting money at such a time—he might refuse——

SHELLEY *and* HARRIET.

SHELLEY Dearest girl, I swear, dearest Harriet—my feelings for you have not changed. My feeling has not changed. What united us, dear Harriet, wasn't love, wasn't passion, what united us was faithful friendship. Friendship united us, friendship shall ever unite us. Oh, Harriet! How I hope, how fervently I hope that you too may find someone towards whom you may feel such overwhelming emotion as I feel for——

MONEYLENDERS. *Moneylender* 1 *wears dark glasses*

78

and is seated in a wheel-chair. MONEYLENDER 2 *wheels the chair.*

M.L. I Godwin is asking for more.

M.L. 2 Money through a sieve.

M.L. I New security. A Mr Shelley.

M.L. 2 Ah. I know the family. Several hundred thousand.

M.L. I Mr. Shelley's wife is in the family way.

M.L. 2 Mrs. Shelley expecting? If it's a boy that will secure the entail. That'll make money easier, ha ha, but not cheaper, ha, ha, but not cheaper.
SHELLEY *and* HARRIET.

SHELLEY Dear Harriet, noble girl, you have not disappointed me. I hoped for calm, for dignity, for honest thinking, and I was not disappointed. Fine, generous girl.

HARRIET (*beginning to whisper to herself through his speeches*) Noble . . . noble . . . generous.

SHELLEY I was not disappointed, fine, fine.

HARRIET Fine, noble.

SHELLEY Dear Harriet! How I hope that you will come to know Mary, as your friend, to love her as your sister—why—why dearest girl, why need we, should we, ever part. Why indeed? What necessity? Why should we not all dwell together?

HARRIET Dwell?

SHELLEY Together, Bound by the sacred ties of friendship, we shall dwell together, you as my sister, Mary as my wife. Would it not be worthy of our pure, disinterested, rational friendship?

HARRIET (*to herself, speaking through his lines*) Pure, Mary, wife, friendships, sister, together, worthy wife, together, worthy, wife——

SHELLEY Shall we be bound by mean conventional thinking? Shall we part? What could be more cruel than to abandon you?

HARRIET (*to herself, speaking through his lines*) Con-con-convention—meanness of convention—meanness of convention? Aban-don, don, child-child-child. . . .

79

SHELLEY Wicked even to consider forgetting those for whom
we feel such friendship, evil to demand that we
should part. Mary shall be to you a sister, a flower,
an angel, a——

HARRIET Oh.

SHELLEY We shall find some sweet spot——

HARRIET Oh! Oh!

SHELLEY And there dwell together.

HARRIET But I'm pregnant.

SHELLEY I know you are. What?

HARRIET I'm pregnant! I'm pregnant!

SHELLEY What?

HARRIET I'm pregnant!

SHELLEY What? What's the matter? I know you are——

GODWIN—MRS GODWIN—MARY.

GODWIN I am Godwin.

MRS G. I am Mrs Godwin.

GODWIN You are not to see him again.

MARY Father!

MRS G. That's right!

MARY You can't prevent me from seeing him.

MRS G. You hear what your father says? I shall lock you in
your room.

MARY Father!

GODWIN I cannot prevent you seeing this man. I rely upon
your filial duty and your own sense of dignity that
you will not allow yourself to act contrary to my
wishes.

SHELLEY *and* HARRIET.

HARRIET Cold! Cruel! Selfish! Hard!

SHELLEY But how can you say—how have I been——

HARRIET I'm pregnant, I'm pregnant!

SHELLEY What difference does that make?

HARRIET You mustn't leave me.

SHELLEY I don't want to leave you. That's just the point. I
don't want to leave you.

HARRIET Please don't leave me, Oh Shelley——

SHELLEY I offer you security, protection; a home with Mary

and me.

HARRIET How did it happen?

SHELLEY A place in my heart, a place in my life——

HARRIET Oh six months ago——

SHELLEY That you may meet someone as worthy of your affection as Mary is of mine.

HARRIET I basked in his love——

SHELLEY Harriet! I want you to live with us, share our life.

HARRIET Oh no!

SHELLEY I will not abandon you.

HARRIET No. No.

SHELLEY I offer you loving friendship.

HARRIET Oh no, not her.

SHELLEY What?

HARRIET Not her.

SHELLEY Why not?

HARRIET No.

SHELLEY You are behaving according to the most irrational ideas of the blindest convention.

HARRIET No.

SHELLEY How can you be so blind? So stupid?

HARRIET But I will soon be brought to bed——

    BAILIFF.

BAILIFF I am a bailiff. I have here a summons to be served upon Percy Bysshe Shelley, to the suit of Charles Charters, coachmaker, to the sum of £633 16s. 6d. Percy Bysshe Shelley.

    HARRIET.

HARRIET (*a cry*) Ah!

    MONEYLENDER.

M.L. 1 And how is the grandfather?

M.L. 2 Ailing.

M.L. 1 Excellent.

    BAILIFF.

BAILIFF £633 16s. 6d.

    HOGG—BAILIFF

HOGG Shelley! Shelley!

BAILIFF Percy Bysshe Shelley?

HOGG Have you seen him?

(BAILIFF *thrusts summons into* HOGG'*s hands*)
What's this?

BAILIFF A summons Mr. Shelley.

HOGG But I'm not Mr Shelley.

BAILIFF You said you were.

HOGG I didn't.

BAILIFF I heard you shouting.

(*Pause*)

HOGG I'm not Mr Shelley.

BAILIFF (*taking back summons*) What you want to shout his
name for then? I summon P. B. Shelley.

(*Enter* SHELLEY, HOGG *heads him off*)

HOGG They're looking for you, they're trying to arrest
you for debt.

SHELLEY I know, I know.

HOGG They'll be watching your home, you mustn't go
back home.

SHELLEY I have no home.

HOGG Go to my lodgings, stay there.

SHELLEY Oh Hogg—(*he pauses, panting*) Oh, Hogg can I ask
you to do something for me?

HOGG Of course, anything.

SHELLEY Go and see Harriet, she's had a son.

HOGG Harriet has had a boy!

SHELLEY Yes, a son. She won't see me, I haven't seen him.
I—Oh! Oh! I love her! I love her desperately, I
love her to distraction!

HOGG Who? Harriet?

SHELLEY No, Mary.

HOGG Shelley, have you thought, have you considered. If
you abandon Harriet——

SHELLEY I'm not abandoning her.

HOGG If you set up an irregular relationship with
Mary——

SHELLEY Well?

HOGG Your writing, your pamphlets, your speeches—who
will listen? You'll be an outlaw, they'll never

82

tolerate you living openly with someone who's not your wife.

SHELLEY But only through Mary can I go on. Mary is to me what I was to Harriet: Wiser! Nobler! Finer!

HOGG What will people say? What will they think?

SHELLEY What does that matter?

SHELLEY *and* HARRIET.

HARRIET Right, you've got a son.

SHELLEY You sound like your sister.

HARRIET My sister, stayed by me, when——

SHELLEY She's a monster of cold, hard, hypocrisy.

HARRIET You talk to me about hypocrisy!

SHELLEY Harriet! Can't we stop this awful, this utterly unworthy bickering? We have striven that our beliefs, our behaviour should be worthy, should be ideal. Isn't this awful quarrelling a betrayal of everything we've achieved together? This is a terrible time for us both, but can't we at least stand by our beliefs and behave with dignity and truth? Don't let's blight and betray all that was good and beautiful in our relationship.

HARRIET You go on about being good and beautiful and at the same time you abandon me and your children, and then expect me, your *wife*, to cohabit with your whore.

SHELLEY Don't utter such cant to me. It is worthy of the most stupid, the lowest—I see now that all this time, while we were together you professed the highest principles—but when they are put to the test——

HARRIET D'you know? D'you know what they are saying? They are saying that Godwin sold her to you.

SHELLEY Harriet!

HARRIET You have given Godwin money! He has sold you Mary!

SHELLEY, MRS GODWIN, CLARE, MARY.

SHELLEY Mary!

MRS G. Mr Shelley!

SHELLEY Mary!

  MARY Shelley!

  MRS G. You can't see her! You're not! Godwin says——
        (SHELLEY *pushes past her to* MARY)

SHELLEY They want to keep us apart my beloved.

  MRS G. Mr Shelley!

SHELLEY But this shall unite us!

  CLARE Laudanum! (*She starts screaming*)
        (MRS GODWIN *screaming*)

SHELLEY We shall escape tyranny!

  MRS G. Godwin! Godwin! Fetch your father.

  CLARE Papa! Papa! Where are you! Mr Shelley's gone
        mad, he'll murder us all!

SHELLEY Let's drink it together, drink it now! Come my
        beloved. Let us die together, death shall unite
        us——

  MARY Stop! Stop! No! Shelley, please——
        (*Enter* GODWIN)

  MRS G. There he is! That's laudanum! Do something! Get
        it off him.

  CLARE Take it from him!
        (*Much screaming and gesticulating in which* GODWIN
        does not take part)

SHELLEY No, no, never, stand back. (*Putting* MARY *behind*
        him he holds the laudanum bottle as he would a
        pistol)
        (MRS GODWIN *collapses in hysterics*)
        Stand back! You shall not touch me! You shall not
        take me alive! Nor her. You shall never part us
        again. Death shall unite us!
        (GODWIN *sits down*)
        (MRS GODWIN's *screaming subsides*)

SHELLEY Mary, my love, let us die together!

  MARY Shelley—Percy!

SHELLEY We shall outwit them!

  MARY I can't.

SHELLEY Mary!

  MARY I cannot, I must not.

SHELLEY You are betraying me.

 MARY I will love you forever. I'll always be faithful.
There shall be no other.

SHELLEY It's not enough. It's not enough.

 MARY Be calm.

SHELLEY If I can't live with you, I must die with you.

 MRS G. Well, did you ever!

GODWIN Be quiet, ma'am.

SHELLEY Mary, oh Mary.

 MARY Be calm my love, I promise you, please be calm.

SHELLEY Oh Mary.

 MARY Be reasonable.

  (MARY *takes the bottle from him*)
  (*Pause*)

GODWIN Mary go to your room.

 MARY But father——

GODWIN Mary.

  (*Exit* MARY)
  And you, Mrs Godwin, go too.

 MRS G. Dearest love, is it safe to leave you with that
madman?

GODWIN And take Clare with you.

 MRS G. But, Mr Godwin——

 CLARE Oh come along, Mama.

 MRS G. Very well. But I must say——

 CLARE Mama!

  (*Exit* MRS GODWIN *and* CLARE)

GODWIN It has clearly not occurred to your deranged senses
how this interruption, caused by your intemperance,
must disturb me in my work. You have
discomposed my peace. Did you, in your irrational
state, pause to consider what would have been the
effect of your extravagant plan? Two bodies, one
may presume, stretched out on my floor. Had you
asked yourself what would be the effect upon my
work of such immoderate behaviour? To take a
longer view: any good I may achieve, any influence
I may possess, depends largely upon my

85

unblemished reputation. If it became known that I was associated with a profligate, that my daughter was openly living with a man who was not her husband, it would utterly destroy any power I may have to promote virtue and progress. I believe that you yourself have some pretension to elevate the state of mankind. But who will listen when an adulterer speaks of virtue?

SHELLEY I love her I——

GODWIN You are beyond reason. Enough of this ridiculous and trivial subject. I would like to speak to you of financial matters.

SHELLEY Financial matters?

GODWIN I have no false pride when I ask for money on behalf of philosophy.

SHELLEY Of course. But I have already negotiated two loans for you.

GODWIN The need is urgent.

SHELLEY Nineteen hundred pounds was not enough?

GODWIN You are heir to a great fortune. You are now the father of a son, your collateral is secure. It should be a simple matter to raise further sums upon expectations such as yours. The interest is naturally high. But we must serve philosophy now must we not? In twenty years it will be too late.

SHELLEY Yes, yes. . . . I will see what I can do, but I have no right to continue pledging my future and my children's future—but I will see what I can do. . . .

GODWIN Please make out any cheques you may have for me in the name of Mr Martin.

SHELLEY Martin?

GODWIN I would not have people know that you are giving me money. I wish you good day. Please leave my house.

(*Exit* SHELLEY)

(GODWIN *sits calmly reading*)

(*Pause*)

(*Knock*)

(*Pause*)

(*Knock repeated*)

I do not wish to be disturbed.

(*Enter* MRS GODWIN)

MRS G. My love, it's important.

(*Pause*)

GODWIN Well?

MRS G. They've eloped, Shelley and Mary. They've gone off together—they left a note.

(*Pause*)

GODWIN Did he leave any m—— . . . message for me?

ACT TWO/SCENE FIVE

Enter SHELLEY *and* MARY.

SHELLEY '. . . the leaves on which we sate,
> And Cythna's glowing arms, and the thick ties
> Of her soft hair, which bent with gathered weight
>> My neck near hers, her dark and deepening eyes,
>> Which, as twin phantoms of one star that lies
> O'er a dim well, move, though the star reposes,
>> Swam in our mute and liquid ecstasies,
> Her marble brow and eager lips like roses,
> With their own fragrance pale, which Spring but
>>> half encloses. . . .

> The beating of our veins one interval
> Made still; and then I felt the blood that burned
>> Within her frame, mingle with mine, and fall
>> Around my heart like fire; and over all
> A mist was spread, the sickness of a deep
>> And speechless swoon of joy. . . .

> . . . What are kisses whose fire clasps
> The failing heart in languishment, or limb
> Twined within limb? Or the quick dying gasps
>> Of the life meeting when the faint eyes swim
>> Through tears of a wide mist boundless and dim,
> In one caress? What is the strong control
>> Which leads the heart that dizzy steep to climb
> Where far over the world those vapours roll,
> Which blend two restless frames in one reposing
>>> soul?'

(*Exit* SHELLEY *and* MARY)

ACT TWO/SCENE SIX

ELIZA *and* WESTBROOK.

ELIZA The streets are empty, there's no one outside. It's too dark to see. No one'll see her going, Pa, no one'll guess.

WESTBROOK Where is she?

(*Enter* HARRIET, *pregnant*)

Right, Harriet. You're not to come back here until it's born and got rid of. Have it under the name of Smith, that clear? Don't let anyone know your real name. I'll not have anyone know my daughter is a bloody whore—eighteen months since she saw her husband and carrying a bastard.

ELIZA I'll look after Ianthe and the baby, if anything should happen.

WESTBROOK Happen?

ELIZA Things can happen in childbirth can't they? I'll see to Ianthe and Charles. Bysshe shan't have the children, I'll see to that.

WESTBROOK Get the man with her bags.

(*Exit* ELIZA)

(*Re-enter* ELIZA *with* PORTER)

Now, my man: Mrs. Smith will tell you where she wants you to take her things. Hurry up and don't let anyone see you.

(PORTER *and* HARRIET *move across the stage. Exit* ELIZA *and* WESTBROOK)

(PORTER *and* HARRIET *go upstage. Exit* PORTER)

(*Pause*)

(*Enter* 1ST GENERAL UTILITY)

1ST. GEN. UT. The Serpentine.

(*Long pause*)

(HARRIET *comes downstage*)

(*Pause*)

89

(*She ties her skirt around her ankles*)
(*Pause*)
(*She lifts her arms and gives an ungainly leap. As she leaps* BLACKOUT)

ACT TWO/SCENE SEVEN

(*Enter* 2 CLERKS)

CLERK I This is the Lord Chancellor's office.

(*Enter* HOGG *and* SHELLEY)

(*Pause*)

(*Enter* ELDON, *the Lord Chancellor*)

ELDON Good morning, George.

CLERK Good morning, my lord.

ELDON Are you ready to begin?

CLERK We are, my lord.

ELDON Very well, let me hear the preamble.

CLERK I (*reads*) Touching the case Westbrook versus
Shelley in which John Westbrook prayeth the Court
of Chancery to appoint him the said John
Westbrook sole guardian of the infants Ianthe Eliza
Shelley girl now aged three and a half or
thereabouts and Charles Bysshe Shelley boy now
aged two years or thereabouts and to restrain and
deprive their father Percy Bysshe Shelley from
taking custody of the said infants.

I, Eldon, Lord Chancellor, having heard the case
argued before me on Friday January 24th 1817 and
having upon that occasion pronounced that I would
consider the case further and would then make
known my decision I have so considered and here
followeth my judgement.

We are quite ready my Lord.

(*As* ELDON *speaks, both* CLERKS *write and their pens
scratch on*)

ELDON This case concerns the principles and conduct in
life of the defendant, the father of these infants, Mr
Shelley. The question at issue is whether the
principles of the father, and the conduct which is

the result of those principles, make him a fit and proper person to have the care of his children, that is to say whether he be allowed to retain his common law rights as a father in his own children. The defendant's principles are set forth in a number of pamphlets and poetical works, including the poetical work 'Queen Mab'. In these works the defendant denies the existence of God the Creator of the universe and denies the truth of the Christian religion, attacks the institution of the Monarchy and questions the processes of the Judiciary, he attacks also established social institutions, such as the institution of Marriage.

As to conduct: Mr Shelley deserted his wife, the mother of these infants, and has since cohabited unlawfully with another woman. Mrs Shelley has lately died.

This is a case where the father's principles cannot be misunderstood. His conduct, which I cannot but consider as highly immoral, is the effect of those principles. Albeit it is conduct which the father represents to himself and others not as conduct to be considered immoral, but as worthy of praise and approbation, to be recommended to others and to be observed in practice.

The father has shown, both in his writings and in his actions and behaviour, that he deems it his duty to recommend these principles to those whose habits and opinions he may take it upon himself to form. To those, as I say, towards whom he wishes to stand in the role of guardian and preceptor. This gentleman's writings plainly show that he regards it as a duty towards such persons to recommend as moral and virtuous conduct which the law calls me to consider as immoral and vicious, conduct which the law animadverts upon as inconsistent with the duty of parents and which the law considers will injure the community.

I cannot therefore consider myself justified in
delivering over these children for their education,
for what is called their care, to Mr Shelley. The
plea of Westbrook is allowed.

(*Exit* ELDON)

(*Exit* CLERKS, *beginning to remove their costumes and
chatting to each other*)

(*Pause*)

(*Through the following the* GENERAL UTILITIES *are
laughing and talking offstage*)

HOGG I suppose you could appeal to the House of Lords.
But I'm afraid—finally the House of Lords is full
of Lord Eldon and his like bent on preserving the
status quo. . . .

SHELLEY Get them.

(*Exit* HOGG)

(*Enter* GENERAL UTILITIES *followed by* HOGG)

SHELLEY Perhaps you should chatter less in that corner and
pay more attention to your job.

GENERAL U. Oh, I'm sorry.

(*Exit* GENERAL UTILITIES)

HOGG I was saying, you could appeal to the House of
Lords——

(*Pause*)

SHELLEY I have no children. He has the power to do it. He
can do it. I have no children. He has spoken and
I have no children.

(*Pause*)

Ianthe.

(*Pause*)

Poor girl, oh poor girl. . . . How could she do it?

(*End of Act Two*)

ACT THREE / SCENE ONE

*A tarpaulin covers the furniture. This low, rocky
mound extends in a curve across the stage.*
TRELAWNY *looking out to sea through his telescope.*
EDWARD WILLIAMS *lying sunning himself.* JANE
WILLIAMS.

TRELAWNY This bay is unbelievable.

EDWARD You should see it just before dawn.

TRELAWNY Uh huh?

EDWARD From Lerici to La Spezia, the whole bay, all the
fishermen out in their boats with torches, you know,
to attract the fish. . . . Extraordinary.

TRELAWNY There's a Portuguese brig putting into La Spezia.

EDWARD Oh . . . where? How can you tell she's Portuguese?

TRELAWNY Double rigging for'ad. Blunt bow.

EDWARD What do you know about ships.

TRELAWNY I'm a sailor.

EDWARD *I'm* a sailor.

> (TRELAWNY *chuckles*)

> Just because Trelawny is a Cornishman who ran
away to sea he thinks he can laugh at the rest of us.

TRELAWNY My dear Edward, you may be able to sail, but
you're not a sailor, not yet.

EDWARD (*good-humoured*) Humph.

> (*Pause*)

JANE Trelawny is a brigand.

TRELAWNY Jane.

JANE Anyone who can put up with Lord Byron's
household at Pisa must be a brigand.

> (*Pause*)

TRELAWNY What a place to build a house.

EDWARD Ah, it's delightful. Shelley and I bathe in front
there by the rocks and Jane tosses us oranges from
the terrace. Shelley says he can feel the spray on

94

his face as he lies in bed. Our room is at the back but we're still only twenty feet from the sea.
(*Pause*)

TRELAWNY How do you find sharing?

EDWARD (*cheery*) A little cramped my dear fellow, only four rooms and what with children and nursemaids. . . . You are a dear, sweet, patient girl, my love. My dear wife says she will make me a roly-poly pudding when she can get at her saucepans.

TRELAWNY You have no saucepans?

EDWARD You're sitting on them my dear fellow.

TRELAWNY Are these your saucepans?

EDWARD Our saucepans, our sofa, our chest of drawers, mirrors and whatnots, bags and baggage odds and ends. Jane has only two pairs of shoes unpacked. We shipped them all from Pisa by sea and there's no room in the house. We came here in such a rush—could only find the one house, so here we all are.

TRELAWNY I can see I'll have to roll up a blanket here by the shore.

EDWARD Oh, there's a sofa inside. I expect you can have that.
(*Pause*)
(EDWARD *shuffles a little*)

TRELAWNY You should have brought some cushions from the house.

JANE Mary doesn't like cushions brought outside.
(*Pause*)

EDWARD (*enjoying the warmth*) Mm. . . .
(*Pause*)

JANE I will make you a roly-poly pudding, dear Edward, when you remember to get me some currants.

TRELAWNY No currants?

EDWARD (*immensely good-humoured*) No road, no shops, Shelley and I got to market at Lerici and not much when we get there. That path you came long by the shore—that's the only way here. We have to carry everything along there by hand. Delightful.

95

TRELAWNY You know when I first met him at your place in Pisa, I couldn't believe—I mean—at home you cannot mention his name in polite society.

(*Pause*)

EDWARD Trelawny, my dear fellow, you are shading me from the sun.

(*Pause*)

TRELAWNY Since he left England—six years ago wasn't it? How much has he had published?

EDWARD He writes a good deal.

(*Pause*)

TRELAWNY Shall we go and have another look at your boat?

EDWARD By all means, yes! Yes!

TRELAWNY I'm not quite happy about——

(*Enter* MARY)

EDWARD Why, Mary! My dear girl! How nice to see you outside. Lovely sunshine! Do you good, dear girl. Ah, you have your parasol. Very wise. Are you feeling a little better after your rest? Would you like me to fetch you a rug?

MARY Thank you, Edward, no.

(*Pause*)

Where is Shelley?

TRELAWNY He went up the hill about an hour ago, he said he wanted to write.

EDWARD When he comes back he'll be in a complete trance.

TRELAWNY A trance?

EDWARD Drunk with poetry. Delightful.

(*Pause*)

TRELAWNY How rich the light is.

EDWARD The real heat is passing.

JANE All golden and warm.

(*Pause*)

MARY The man who built this house was a lunatic.

TRELAWNY Mm?

MARY He is confined in a madhouse. He uprooted all the olive trees on the hillside behind the house and planted English trees.

96

TRELAWNY English trees?

MARY Chestnut, ilex.

EDWARD To the Italians that would be lunatic.

MARY Well, he's in a madhouse.

(*Pause*)

MARY Our maid says she cannot find our teapot.

EDWARD Teapot?

MARY (*speaking to* JANE) She says you took it and did not return it.

JANE Oh? I don't recall.

EDWARD I'm sure Jane would return it, wouldn't you, dear girl?

(*Pause*)

JANE Where would I take it? There's only our room.

MARY I'm sure I have no idea where you would have taken it.

EDWARD I do assure you, Mary dear, it's not in our room. I haven't seen it anywhere.

(*Pause*)

Shall we go and look for the teapot? Yes? A teapot hunt!

(*Enter* SHELLEY)

(MARY *does not react or move*)

Ah, my dear fellow. . . . Ah. . . .

(SHELLEY *lies down*)

(*Very long pause*)

JANE 'Now all the tree tops lay asleep,
  Like green waves on the sea,
And still as in the silent deep
  The ocean woods may be.
How calm it was!—The silence there
  By such a chain was bound
That even the busy woodpecker
  Made stiller by her sound
The inviolable quietness. . . . '

(*Long pause*)

(SHELLEY *lays a piece of paper by* JANE)

SHELLEY (*to* JANE) Here is a poem for you.

(*Pause*)
(SHELLEY *exits*)
(MARY *rises*)
(MARY *takes paper from* JANE)
(*Pause*)
(JANE *exits*)
(MARY *is about to follow*)
(*A baby crying within*)

MARY Nurse! Nurse! Is that the baby? Is he all right?
(*Exit* MARY *toward the house*)
(*Pause*)

EDWARD Mary hasn't been well. . . . She's er . . . she's in the
family way . . . we thought—last week we thought
she might lose the baby—it was an awful journey
from Pisa—and the house hunting—little upsets,
little upsets. You see, perhaps we can help in some
way. Oh, very fortunate we're here.
(*Pause*)

TRELAWNY The baby—I mean the baby that was crying—is he
their only child?

EDWARD Lord Byron hasn't told you? They have had four
children.

TRELAWNY Dead?

EDWARD I believe the first was a little girl, died almost as
soon as she was born. The second, William, he was
spared longest. Oh, they deeply loved him. A little
girl, Clara. She died in Mary's arms in Venice
while Shelley was trying to find a doctor. William
died last year in Florence.

TRELAWNY Poor Mary.
(*Enter* SHELLEY *and* JANE)

SHELLEY 'The deep recesses of her odorous dwelling
Were stored with magic treasures—sounds of air,
Which had the power all spirits of compelling,
Folded in cells of crystal silence there'.

'And there lay Visions swift, and sweet, and quaint
Each in its thin sheath, like a crysalis,
Some eager to burst forth, some weak and faint

98

With the soft burthen of intensest bliss.'
'And odours in a kind of aviary
     Of ever-blooming Eden-trees she kept,
Clipped in a floating net, a love-sick fairy
     Had woven from dew-beams while the moon yet
                                    slept.'

Trelawny, have you seen our new boat?

TRELAWNY Yes, I have.

SHELLEY 'She had a boat which some say Vulcan
wrought——'

TRELAWNY She strikes me as shallow-draughted.

EDWARD Shallow-draughted!

TRELAWNY She looks to be riding very high in the water. How
does she handle in the wind?

EDWARD My dear fellow, with your knowledge of boats—can
you be serious? She's sublime, she goes like a bird.

TRELAWNY How much ballast is she carrying?

EDWARD Two tons.

TRELAWNY Two tons for a boat that size?

EDWARD Two tons of iron ballast on the keel, it's just to
steady her.

TRELAWNY So I'm right then. She's not steady.

EDWARD She sails like a witch.

SHELLEY 'This boat she moored upon her fount, and lit
     A living spirit within all its frame'——

EDWARD She goes like a witch. Doesn't she, Shelley?

SHELLEY Edward and I plan a great voyage. The
Mediterranean is a puddle, a mere puddle.

EDWARD A mere puddle.

SHELLEY Hah ha! The Atlantic: the rollers, the breakers.

TRELAWNY You fine weather sailors. This sea is treacherous:
sudden storms. I hope you're both good swimmers.

EDWARD I can. Shelley can't.

TRELAWNY Shelley can't swim! But——

SHELLEY 'And ever down the prone vale, like a cloud
     Upon the stream of wind, the pinnace went'——

TRELAWNY Shelley, forgive me, but——

SHELLEY 'Now lingering on the pools, in which abode

99

            The calm and darkness of the deep content
            In which they paused'——
            (*Pause*)

TRELAWNY You ought to learn to swim.

SHELLEY Teach me.

TRELAWNY Very well.

EDWARD I took him on last week. He threw himself on to the bottom and just lay there.

TRELAWNY Lay there?

EDWARD He simply threw himself into 12 feet of water, went straight to the bottom and lay there. I had the devil of a time pulling him out.
            (*Pause*)

TRELAWNY Let's go and have a look at that sail.

EDWARD I'm not quite happy about it either, my dear fellow.

SHELLEY (*gay*) Edward is not happy, we have put in two reefs.
            'The water flashed like sunlight by the prow'.
            (*Exit* TRELAWNY *and* EDWARD *followed by*
            SHELLEY *and* JANE)
            (*Pause*)
            (*Enter* MARY *she stands watching them. Pause. She reads the paper aloud*)

MARY (*very cool, light tone*) This is the poem he wrote for Jane:
            'She left me, and I stayed alone
            Thinking over every tone
            Which, though silent to the ear,'
            (*Enter* SHELLEY)
            'The enchanted heart could hear'

                              —charming fancy!

            'Thinking over every tone
            Which, though silent to the ear,
            The enchanted heart could hear'——
            Ah, Shelley's imagination! I wonder did Jane's enchanted heart also hear those silent tones?
            'And feeling ever—oh, too much!—
            The soft vibration of her touch,

As if her gentle hand, even now,
Lightly trembled on my brow;'
Or was it you who were trembling?

SHELLEY (*having rejected many thoughts: 'It is not true', 'you
must not belittle me and my work so'. 'How can she
so demean herself?' etc. . . .*) Poor Mary.
(*Slightest pause*)

MARY Please do not say 'Poor Mary'. Please do *not* say
'Poor Mary'. . . . It will be five o'clock at home.
They will be serving afternoon tea. Ladies in hats
with kid gloves on their laps. Ha, ha, kid gloves . . .
and lace table cloths, and a silver tea service. . . .
(*Pause*)

SHELLEY Would you like some tea?

MARY No thank you.
(*Pause*)

SHELLEY There is nothing, nothing that vulgar minds would
call something, between Jane and me.

MARY She strokes your head, however . . . tremblingly.

SHELLEY But if there were, Mary, your true, your noble
nature would tell you that I would not deceive you.

MARY Your noble nature would tell me when you had
gone too far. You would tell me then.

SHELLEY (*pause: putting from his mind the feeling of distaste at
the vulgarity of new words: these thoughts pass
through his mind; they are not to be spoken:
You know my values, dear Mary, I have striven, I
have striven passionately—yes, I know the world
thinks physical love a wicked and guilty thing. This
is so terrible that—but for your sake I respect the
values of the world. Nevertheless, for me there is
no dividing line between a moment's intense
spiritual communication and a lifetime of physical
love. So how can I swear that I have not been
unfaithful to you?*)
Too far?

MARY (*Pause: Thoughts, not to be spoken:
Oh come, this is nonsense. Think no more of it, so*

you sit with Jane in the woods and she strokes your brow.)

I remember a poem you wrote in a similar situation: Emilia. . . . You remember Emilia? Another young woman for whom Shelley conceived one of his emotional attachments. Oh, purely platonic. We cannot say it was a corporal relationship for after all Emilia was locked up in a convent was she not? How noble, intelligent and pure she was! How you poured forth your soul in song!—'I never was. . . .'

SHELLEY (*interrupting*) Please don't quote that poem.

MARY You don't like it any more?

SHELLEY I can't bear to think of it now.

MARY (*slight pause*) I have been wondering what I shall have made with that pretty piece of silk I bought in Pisa. . . . (*Pause*) And my grey shoes need mending. I wonder if one can get shoes mended in this abominable place.

SHELLEY There is a cobbler at Sarzano.

MARY Oh yes, a cobbler in Sarzano.

SHELLEY Mary, you aren't well, you had a haemorrhage last week. . . . I think when you're a little better and a little stronger you'll see things more in perspective and you'll be happier.

MARY Oh, I'm feeling particularly well today. I see things with extraordinary clarity. I know when I will be happier.

SHELLEY When we leave this house.

MARY It is not precisely the house I object to, dear Percy, 'standing with its feet in the sea' which you find so beautiful and romantic, whereas it is merely damp. No, it is the remoteness, the sharing a kitchen with Jane—Incidently they have taken our teapot and presumably broken it. Sharing a house with that couple, and peeling walls.

SHELLEY The teapot?

MARY The same.

SHELLEY When did you see it last?

MARY Oh, I don't know, last night?

SHELLEY But, Mary, we had it at breakfast—I took it on to the terrace.

MARY Did you.

SHELLEY It must still be there. Shall I tell them?

MARY If you wish.

SHELLEY (*calling*) Jane! Jane!

(*Enter* JANE)

MARY It seems I made a mistake. Shelley says our teapot is on the terrace.

JANE I beg your pardon?

SHELLEY The teapot's on the terrace. I'm so sorry, it's all my fault.

JANE (*not knowing whether to be sour, but deciding to smile, though grimly*) I see, thank you.

(*Exit* JANE)

SHELLEY Lie down, my love, and put your head in my lap. There. . . . Edward and Tre are clambering all over the boat. What a dear fellow Edward is. . . . What do you think of Trelawny? . . . I like him. . . . How few friends we have—four perhaps in England and here—(*pause*). . . . They'd drive us off the face of the earth if they could. . . . I can feel their hate even here. What's left? Fame? That makes you smile. Seeking for sympathy amongst people you have never met, will never know, what a feeble way of assuaging the love in us . . . and even that is beyond me. Nobody reads my poems. Once I wanted to transform the world. Now. . . ? Now. . . ?

(*Pause*)

MARY Oh my dearest, I'm so unhappy, I'm so unhappy.

SHELLEY I know, my love. I know.

(*Pause*)

MARY Shelley.

SHELLEY Yes, love?

MARY When we—came together——

SHELLEY Yes?

103

MARY What did you tell Harriet?
(*Slight pause*)

SHELLEY I told her what you meant to me, how much I loved you. I reminded her of our beliefs, hers and mine; and our philosophy, our common values on which our marriage was based. That though I held her, and would always hold her, in the deepest affection, yet I loved you.

MARY She still loved you.

SHELLEY But you know very well, Mary, that I loved you.

MARY But she still loved you.
(*Pause*)

SHELLEY But the partner who, alas, still loves cannot hold the other, for their love becomes a chain, and soon it'll become hatred.
(*Pause*)
Between Jane and me, dearest Mary, there is nothing more than that intense sympathy people sometimes feel towards each other perhaps only for a few moments, when sympathetic natures reach towards each other in kindness.

MARY Kindness and sympathy you do not get from your wife.
(*Pause*)
(SHELLEY *doesn't speak, partly because it's true, partly because he sees she is deliberately torturing herself*)
Remember Emilia? Remember?
'Sleep, the fresh dew of languid love, the rain Whose drops quench kisses till they burn again.'

SHELLEY Not that poem, please.

MARY Ha Ha! Emilia!
'And we will talk, until thought's melody Become too sweet for utterance, and it die In words, to live again in looks, which dart With thrilling tone into the voiceless heart, Harmonizing silence without a sound.
Our breath shall intermix, our bosoms bound,

104

And our veins beat together: and our lips
With other eloquence than words, eclipse
The soul that burns between them, and the wells
Which boil under our being's inmost cells
The fountains of our deepest life, shall be
Confused in Passion's golden purity.'
Naughty Emilia. You carol on about Passion's
golden purity and finally you discover she's a
hard-headed little slut.

SHELLEY Mary!

MARY Does it still hurt so much?

SHELLEY Yes.

MARY Ah!

SHELLEY I was foolish. I was blind.

MARY But, my darling, you are always foolish, you are
always blind. You are always——

SHELLEY No! The moment of truth is the moment of
experience. When two souls reach out to each other.
As true, valuable and beautiful as a lifetime of living.
Oh it's hard that people may retreat, may not
maintain that ecstasy. But if it's truly felt it remains.
Our deepest, purest moments, most powerfully
endure.
(*Pause*)
What is it?

MARY I don't feel well.

SHELLEY Is it the baby?

MARY I don't know.

SHELLEY Let me carry you to the house.

MARY Just a moment.
(*Pause*)

MARY Oh, Shelley, what have we come to? Six years since
we left home: rattling round Italy—Venice, Rome,
Florence, Pisa, Clara, William, and now here; why
are we here?
You get out of your carriage at Lerici and grope
along the shore. Mountains one side, sea the other,
and then no more path, nothing. It's the end of the

world. What next?

Oh, for the smell of clean furniture and lavender and fresh tea and cushions. . . . Another child into this hell. Carry it, bear it, nurse it, kill it. Do you know why they die, Percy? Because we have no home. We run from place to place. And little children want peace; they want peace. Their little stomachs get upset and they die. . . .

SHELLEY Let's go into the house.

MARY I hate that house! I hate that house! Are you in love with her Percy? She's so stupid. You put things on to them, Percy, that they haven't got. You see it all as brave, virtuous, noble, strong. . . . And we cannot go back. Percy can't we go back? Ah, the abomination! You thought you could change the world and here I am tied to you. You write and no one reads. No one reads! A great prophet. At home they pick up your books with tongs. And you thought you could change the world. Look at the misery you've dragged me into, sitting here at the end of the world, waiting to miscarry.

(*Pause*)

I think I'm——

SHELLEY Come.

MARY No, no.

SHELLEY Mary, you must go in.

MARY No.

SHELLEY You must lie down.

MARY Don't touch me!

(*Pause*)

(*Enter* EDWARD *and* TRELAWNY)

EDWARD Is anything wrong? We thought we heard Mary, er, calling.

SHELLEY She must go into the house.

MARY I won't go into the house.

SHELLEY She's had another haemorrhage.

MARY I'm not, I haven't, don't touch me.

(*Pause*)
They all think you're wonderful, look at their eyes,
how they despise me. But I'll tell them. Don't go,
Edward! You mustn't go. I'm going to show you.
Flesh and blood cannot stand it. I will not stand it.

SHELLEY Dearest Mary, you cannot shake me.

MARY Don't look at me like that. Don't look at me like
that.
(*Pause*)
Edward, what do you think of Shelley and Jane
running off into the woods together?

EDWARD Er—I beg your pardon?

MARY He writes her love poems.

EDWARD Oh, my dear girl, that doesn't mean anything, he's
a poet.

MARY You're very foolish. He left his first wife didn't he?
And Jane is so stupid. I warn you Shelley. If you go
on like this with Jane—I cannot bear it. Oh no. (*Light
and cold*) I shall not. There are ways and ways.

EDWARD What do you mean, my dear girl?

MARY Shelley knows what I mean. So does Trelawny.

SHELLEY Stop behaving like this.

MARY You will be sorry when it is too late.

SHELLEY Your threats of suicide will merely serve to make
me lie to you. I shall by every means prevent your
suicide, and prevent it if need be by lying.

MARY Don't be so savage, I am ill.

SHELLEY I am not being savage, dear Mary, I am being
truthful. The only way to restore trust between us,
Mary, is to remove all coercion, all threats. Forgive
all, accept all.

MARY Oh, beautiful! Beautiful!

SHELLEY You are beyond reason.

MARY Reason! Is that what you said to Harriet?
(*Slight pause*)
Promise me you will love me for ever.

SHELLEY I cannot promise that. And if you were in your
right mind you would not ask me.

MARY Promise me you will love me for ever or I will kill myself.

SHELLEY Very well, I will love you for ever.

MARY Swear it.

SHELLEY If you wish.

MARY Swear it on the Bible.

SHELLEY Very well.

MARY Edward! You have a Bible, have you not?

EDWARD Er, yes.

MARY Fetch it.

EDWARD Eh?

MARY Fetch it.

>(EDWARD *goes*)
>
>(*Long pause*)
>
>(*Re-enter* EDWARD *with Bible which he gives to* MARY)
>
>(*Pause*)

MARY What does a Bible mean to him?

>(MARY *begins to weep*)

SHELLEY Mary, dearest, dearest Mary, the only thing that can dissolve this misery is love.

MARY Love!

SHELLEY Love and acceptance.

>(*Pause*)

MARY Edward, don't go.

EDWARD I'm, er—I will come back.

>(*Exit* EDWARD)

MARY I know why this sorrow is upon us.

SHELLEY It's upon us because we won't accept the cold cruelty of the world and people hate me for fighting it, so they have banished me.

MARY No, it's because you think and act the way you do. They punish you because you are wrong. They are right and you are wrong.

SHELLEY No.

MARY We are paying now for Harriet's misery.

SHELLEY What?

MARY We are paying now for Harriet's misery.

SHELLEY Not a day passes but I am tortured by the memory of Harriet.

MARY Yes, because you killed her.

(*Pause*)

You sent her to her death. That's why we're so unhappy. We're paying now. You abandoned Harriet and she killed herself.

SHELLEY You are distorting the facts.

MARY You killed Harriet.

SHELLEY My sin towards Harriet, my only sin, was in ever marrying her. I should never have married her. I did not abandon her, I gave her money, she had her children and her family, I besought, I implored her to make her home with us. What more could I do that would not have distorted and destroyed our lives? Finally Harriet killed herself not because of my fault but because she was pregnant by another man and driven from home. It was the cruelty of her family and her own weakness.

MARY You killed her, that is why we are unhappy.

(*Pause*)

SHELLEY So at last even you, abandon me.

MARY And I warn you: if you leave me, I shall kill myself too.

(*Pause*)

Trelawny, will you take me into the house.

(*Exit* TRELAWNY *and* MARY)

(*Long pause*)

(*Exit* SHELLEY *in the opposite direction*)

ACT THREE/SCENE TWO

TRELAWNY It was not long after that Shelley and Edward
Williams were returning from Leghorn by sea, in
their boat. They were caught in a storm and failed
to return to Lerici where Mary and Jane waited in
the most intense anxiety. At first we allowed
ourselves to hope that they might have been swept
across to Corsica and I rode up and down the coast
trying to get news of them.

But pieces of the wreckage of their boat were found
and then, in a few days, the two bodies were cast
ashore near Via Reggio, and were hurriedly
shovelled into the sand. We wanted to transfer the
remains to Rome for proper burial. But the laws of
quarantine were strict and we could not proceed
with this plan. We therefore resolved to burn the
bodies on the beach.

I made my preparations: ordering a cradle, or
furnace, of iron to burn the bodies in, and I
procured honey, wine and salt to burn with the
bodies. Everything being ready we sailed from
Leghorn in the *Bolivar*, Lord Byron's yacht, on
Tuesday August the 13th, 1822.

When we arrived at Via Reggio we were met by the
Officer of Health and a troop of soldiers who were
to help us in our task. They had with them long-
handled tongs, nippers, poles, iron hooks and pikes
for we were forbidden to touch the bodies directly
for fear of infection.

As to the place where they were buried: to one
side was the Mediterranean Sea with the islands of
Gorgona, Capraia, Elba and Corsica, on the other
side a flat, sandy wilderness, uncultivated,

uninhabited and beyond: the mountains capped in white marble.

It was nearly an hour before we found where he was buried. As they were digging a spade struck the skull, the body was soon uncovered. His dress and linen had become black and the body was in a state of putridity and very offensive, the flesh was of a dingy blue.

We made a fire and placed the body in the furnace, and as it burned the oil and salt which I poured on the fire made the flames glisten and quiver. The heat from the sun and fire was so intense that the atmosphere was tremulous and wavy.

The corpse fell open and the heart was laid bare. Where it had been struck by the mattock, the frontal bone of the skull fell off and, the back of the head resting on the red hot bottom bars of the furnace, the brains seethed.

The body was a long time consuming, the fierce fire kept up and the largest bones were reduced to white cinders and nothing perfectly distinguishable —but the heart, though bedded in fire, would not burn—and after waiting an hour, continually adding fuel, we gave over, all exclaiming it will not burn. There was a bright flame all round it caused by the moisture still flowing from it—and on removing the furnace nearer the sea to cool the iron I took the heart in my hand to examine it. I sprinkled it with water, but it was still so hot as to burn my hand badly, and a quantity of this oily liquid still flowed from it.

We now collected the ashes, placed them in a wooden box made for the purpose and shipped it aboard Lord Byron's schooner. We then weighed anchor and set sail for Leghorn.

THE END

DATE DUE

RETURNED	
APR 27 '80	
RETURNED	